SP Pvt. Ltd.

High Mortality of Children
Some Facts

by

Pritee Singh

2017

Studium Press (India) Pvt. Ltd.

High Mortality of Children
Some Facts

ISBN: 978-93-85046-02-5

Published by:

Studium Press (India) Pvt. Ltd.
4735/22, 2nd Floor, Prakash Deep Building
(Near Delhi Medical Association),
Ansari Road, Darya Ganj, New Delhi-110 002
Tel.: + 91-11-43240200-15 (15 lines); Fax: 91-11-43240215
E-mail: studiumpress@gmail.com

Printed in India

About the Author

Pritee Singh

Pritee Singh is Assistant Professor in Department of Statistics, Institute of Science, Nagpur. She has also served as Assistant Professor in the Department of Statistics, Government Vidharbh Institute of Science and Humanities, Amravati and Sydenham College of Commerce and Economics, Mumbai before being transferred to Nagpur. She got M.Sc. and Ph. D. from Department of Statistics, Sant Gadge Baba Amravati University, Amravati. She has graduated with Mathematics, Statistics and Computer Science. She has also obtained Post Graduate Diploma in Quality Control and Reliability from All India institute of Management studies, Chennai. She has published research papers in the International Journals like JTT, IAPQR and JRSS etc. and has experience of many years of doing U.G. and P.G. examination work for R.T.M. Nagpur University, S.G.B. Amravati University and Mumbai University. Her area of research interest includes Inference and Population Science. She has completed 01 Major Research Project funded by DST, New Delhi and 01 Major Research Project funded by University Grants Commission, New Delhi.

Preface

Melghat region is a part of Amravati District in the North Eastern Maharashtra. This region is hilly and is mostly covered with dense forest. The population of this region is almost rural and tribal and it mainly consists of "Korkus". This region has a severe problem of malnutrition and a large number of children have died and are still dying due to this. To review and understand, as well as suggest some solutions to this problem, is an urgent need of today. It will be really fruitful if a statistician tackles and investigates this problem and suggests some remedies. Considering these points the present work has been done. This work intends to do something for the society and not for simply being kept in the libraries after performing some mathematical juggleries.

The study of this subject requires the knowledge of five subjects namely Sociology Economic, Home Science and Medical Science as well as above all the knowledge of Statistics. Here, a deep knowledge of statistical demography was also needed. Thus, the considered research problem is in fact an inter- disciplinary work which required the knowledge of several subjects and so it was a difficult task.

The present book is divided into seven chapters. The first chapter is introductory. The second chapter provides the general information, the research work already undertaken by other researchers as well as the research methodology used for the present book. In the third chapter, some government data has been collected from different government sources and statistically analysed to prepare the basis for the study and to assess the original situation. The Chapters 4, 5 and 6 present the analysis of general profile of the respondents, economical factors and demographical factors, respectively on the basis of the data collected by the me. Here, some statistical models have also been developed. All these chapters contain the findings based on the analysis done by author. The last chapter provides the conclusions as well as some recommendations to solve the problem in Melghat region. At the end, a list of references has been given and a sample copy of the format of questionnaire used for collecting the data has been enclosed in the form of Appendix *"A"*.

Pritee Singh, M.Sc., Ph.D.
Department of Statistics
Institute of Science, Nagpur

Table of Contents

1

Introduction

Statistics is one of the oldest sciences known to human society. Its existence can be seen during the period of *Ramayana* as well as *Mahabharata* (see Prabhu Ajgaonkar (1995). Godambe (1976)). Modern theory of statistics, also known as theoretical statistics has developed during the mid seventeenth century with the search of "Theory of Probability" and "Theory of games and chance". The French mathematician Pascal solved the famous problem of points posed by the gambler Chevalier De-Mere, after lengthy correspondence with another mathematician P. Fermat of his country. His study of this problem laid the foundation of the theory of probability which has now become the backbone of the modern theory of Statistics. Also, during the same century, the concept of vital Statistics was developed by Captain John Graunt of London, known as father of Vital Statistics. He was the first man to study the statistics of births and deaths, computations of mortality tables and calculation of expected life at different ages by considering a number of persons. The father of statistics Sir R.A. Fisher, placed Statistics on a very sound footing by applying it to various diversified fields like genetics, biometry, education, agriculture, etc. He also pioneered the study of "Analysis of Variance" and "Design of Experiments", apart from pioneering as well as introducing the concepts of Point Estimation, Fiducial Inference and Exact sampling distributions.

The science of population studies or Demography (see Bartholomew (1982), Cox (1970), Keyfitz (1977) and Spiegelman (1969)) has also played an important role in understanding and solving the problems of the society. In fact, Demography means the quantitative and qualitative study of the population. This topic will be further discussed in later sections.

Statistics has seen a lot of theoretical development during the last two centuries. A number of researchers have contributed significantly to develop the theoretical statistics in various branches of it. The different theoretical branches such as Theory of sample survey (see Chaudhari and Vos (1988), Cochran (1988), Mukhopadhyay (1998), Murthy (1977) and Sukhatme *et al.* (1984)), Statistical Inference (see Lehmann (1986 a,b), Ferguson (1967) and Zacks (1971)), Design of Experiment (see Chakraborty (1962), Das and Giri (1979), John (1971), Montgomery (1976) and Pearce (1984)), Operations Research (sec Churchman *et al.* (1957) and Taha (1982)), Multivariate analysis (Anderson (1983), Morrison (1976) and Johnson and Wychern (1992)), Bayesian Analysis (see Berger (1985), Ferguson (1967) and Box and Tiao (1973)), Life Testing and Reliability Theory (see Barlow and Proschan (1985), Lawless (1982), Bain and Engelhardt (1991) and Cox and Oakes (1984)) and Quality Control (Montgomery (1985) and Ott (1975)), etc. are being applied and used in every walk of our day to day life.

Thus, the research and development of the subject has been more or less theoretical only and least care has been taken to apply for solving the problems of the society. Not many applied research has come recently dealing with the day to day problems of mankind. It therefore, becomes the duty of the applied statistician to use the knowledge of theories of statistics to search for the solutions of the real problems in the form to uplift their living standards. For this, the problems related to society must be undertaken as a research problem and concrete solutions must be suggested to answer the causes and reasons involved there in. This will also help to popularize the subject in the society as well as the people can understand the usefulness of the subject. Recently, the Indian Society of Probability and Statistics, India has started a similar type of research activity of applied work to inculcate the concept of applying knowledge of Statistics for solving the problems of society (See Gore (2001)). These researches may not involve mathematical rigor but suggestions to help to improve the life of millions for whom the world is so worried.

During the last decade, the concept of interdisciplinary work has emerged. A number of international scientists have advocated for this at different levels and some good research works have also been carried out in various disciplines. The National Assessment and Accreditation Council, Bangalore has also very strongly weighted for this. Moreover, University Grants Commission, New Delhi has also recommended such kind of curriculum in every subject in general and Statistics in particular. Considering above facts the author has been motivated to undertake this topic which applies statistics in solving the problems of society as well as an inter-disciplinary work.

1.1. DEMOGRAPHY

Demography or population studies literally mean the quantitative and qualitative study of the population. "Demo" means the people or population at large and "graphy" means a technique of projecting the picture of the same. In other words, "Demography is a science or a technique leading to the analysis of the population". If the features of the population *e.g.*, sex ratio, survival, etc. are looked from biological perspective, the subject becomes a branch of Biometry. On the other hand, if the features of a population are considered as the outcome of a particular socio-economic process then the study of the population should be based on socio-economic considerations and as such it may be viewed as a branch of Sociometry. But strictly speaking, the scope of Demography is the analysis of a population, which being both qualitative as well as quantitative in nature. Hence, the subject acquires the status of an independent discipline, covering the areas of Biology, Sociology and Economics while using Statistical Methodologies. Here, it is looked from statistical point of view. In other words, analyze the data by employing appropriate probabilistic techniques. Briefly, it can be concluded that the application of probabilistic technique in Biology leads to the formation of Biometry, in sociology to sociometry and in Demography to Demomtry. However, the scope of the subject which the author envisages to present, being not comprehended fully by probabilistic techniques only, while there exists a major coverage of the subject with descriptive or qualitative methods.

The population of an area increases by births and decreases by deaths if it is assumed that the area is not affected by immigration and emigration. The difference between the births and deaths is called Natural increase in the population. For a study of population growth one should have the following information:

i) The number of events that happen,

ii) The population to which the events occur,

iii) The interval of time during which the events occur.

As the events of births and deaths occur continuously as well as simultaneously in the population, the task of study of the population becomes difficult.

1.2. VITAL STATISTICS

Another way of studying the characteristics of population is known as vital statistics. It is defined as that branch of Biometry which deals with data and the laws of human mortality, morbidity and demography. The term vital statistics refers to the numerical data or the techniques used in the analysis of the data pertaining to vital events occurring in the given section of the population. By vital events, we mean such events of human life as fertility and mortality (births and deaths), marriages, divorce, separation, adoptions, legitimateness, etc. and events which are deemed reportable by local health authorities. The main uses of vital statistics include:

1) The population estimation and forecasting,
2) Analysis of health trends,
3) Program Planning, monitoring and evaluation,
4) Operational and administrative decision making,
5) Providing indices for measuring health and diseases in a community,

6) Providing tools and methods for measuring and comparing morbidity, mortality, fertility, etc. of one city or state or country or region and with that of the other cities or states or countries or regions and with respect to religion, caste, creed or community.

7) Providing for chances of survival in a particular disease and expectancy of life at birth or any age.

8) Information regarding all possible factors contributing to deaths in various ages which is indispensable tool in all life insurance schemes in the form of Actuarial Science.

The vital statistics data are usually obtained by the following methods: (i) Census, (ii) Registration of vital events, (iii) Sample registration system, (iv) Notification of disease, (v) Hospital records, (vi) Disease registers, (vii) Record linkage, (viii) Epidemiologic surveillance, (ix) Health service records, (x) Environmental health data, (xi) Health manpower data and (xii) Population surveys.

In vital statistics, the interest is in measuring health and disease conditions, comparing them with other times and places and drawing logical interpretations to help us in program planning, monitoring and evaluation. There are some tools for measuring these vital events. These tools are -

(i) Rate, ii) Ratio and iii) Proportion.

Further, the rates are also defined in following ways (see Mukhopadhyay (1999))

(i) Crude, ii) Specific and iii) Standardized.

1.3. NEED OF PRESENT STUDY

The news papers from 1974 onwards have reported that the highest percentages of severe malnutrition among 1 to 5 years old tribal children has been observed in Melghat region in Amravati district which also had the lowest percentage of children with adequate nutrition. This has raised a question to search the problem behind this. A study can be undertaken which may throw light on the economical and demographical factors of that region which are responsible for the malnutritional status of the children. It must be appropriate in the 21st Century that a serious attention must be paid on the problems of tribal people in general and Melghatis in particular, since they are really backward in a number of ways. Most of the tribal are still at the stage of development as socially as well as economically. The information on different aspects which are taken here will not only serve as guide for specific intervention program for the upliftment of these tribes but will also help in monitoring the situation over a period of time. This present study will bring out the information regarding nutritional problems of the children of Melghat. It will also enlighten the economical and demographical conditions of Melghat which may be responsible for the nutritional status of the children and consequently leads to their death.

1.4. PROBLEMS UNDER INVESTIGATION

The role of Statistics as envisaged earlier is multifarious in nature. The growing importance of statistics as an application oriented science cannot be discounted. Rather, Statistics and its applications for decision making, proper problem formation, analysis of causes and effects on various events have a great importance in the present socio-economic as well as technical and industrial planning. Most of the institutions prefer a more precisely defined and highly reliable data which cannot be acquired without application of statistical techniques.

Statistics as a tool of research and method of investigation is thus of great importance. Many research problems in socio-economics and science can be rightly defined and understood if tested with the help of statistical techniques. Hence, applying statistical techniques to study inter-disciplinary issues is more scientific as well as reliable system.

Social problems can be rightly studied with the help of statistical techniques. Issues related with population dynamics, demographic structure and relative changes in the birth and death rates as well as composition of population have great implications in National Planning. If these issues are addressed rightly by applying suitable statistical techniques *i.e.* Demographical methods, then the level of accuracy can be adequately enhanced. The estimates become more precise, accurate and close to realistic data. Hence, applying statistical techniques for analysis, synthesis and prognosis of different research problems in society is appropriately justified.

The present topic of study is a critical analysis of causes of increase in death rate due to malnutrition of infants and children in Melghat region. Malnutrition being a widespread phenomenon in the tribal area, it is necessary to pay an urgent attention to this grave social ailment. The reasons of malnutrition being diversified in nature and unless and until specific cause effect relationship is established suitable remedy to eradicate it cannot be instituted. Though malnutrition is a global phenomenon, the reasons vary from place to place and region to region. To identify and locate the set of specific reasons is a must for introducing a suitable mechanism. Hence, use of statistical techniques for study of malnutrition and causes there off in Melghat region is justified.

1.5. PRESENT WORK

The book consists of seven chapters. The present chapter gives the general idea of the statistics/Demography as a subject. A brief discussion on Demography and vital statistics has also been presented. The need of present study as well as problem under investigation has been explained to understand the importance of this study and to identify the actual problem under investigation. At the end of this chapter, the details of the complete book, briefing the work of each chapter have been provided in the form of present work.

The second chapter contains a review of literature and research methodology. In this chapter, first of all the area under study, its geographical location, other important characteristics, information about population of the area have been given. The tribes are the main constituents of the population in the region under study and in the earlier study on tribes, economical status of tribes have been discussed. In this chapter, the meaning of malnutrition as well as the disease caused by it has been discussed to make the basis of the present work. Similarly, the malnutrition in children has also been discussed. The research methodology used for present work has been given at the end.

In the third chapter, a pilot work has been done before studying the actual data collected by author. The data related to different types of malnutrition, in the different age group of children, number of deaths due to malnutrition, etc. are collected by government health department have been statistically analyzed and the inference has been drawn about the different schemes run by government and its effectiveness. At the beginning of this chapter, the different schemes offered by government have been briefly discussed.

The general profile of the respondents has been presented in chapter 4. In fact, this chapter gives first part of the data collected by author and its analysis. Here the questions regarding age, sex, family size, educational qualification, type of houses they live in, age at marriage and their marital status, etc. have been studied and a probability distribution of family size has been developed.

Economic status plays a very important role to understand the economic status of a society. This economic status depends on the geographical situation and the

Forest in Melghat (*Source* – Nayak, 2012)

Forest in Melghat (*Source* – Nayak, 2012)

prosperity is the result of resource available in the region. The economic factors like occupation, annual income, income of husband, income of wife, income of children, their domestic animals and monthly expenditure on various heads and details of government aids, etc. have been statistically analyzed in chapter 5.

The sixth chapter deals with demographical factors. The factors like birth and place of birth, vaccination, the family planning information, its knowledge and source have been considered. The diet, its type, breast feeding and number of births as well as deaths during the last five years have also been considered and studied to clarify the cause of deaths of children. Also, probability distributions are suggested for some factors.

The last chapter provides our conclusions after doing the statistical study of the whole problem in the earlier chapters. Also, some recommendations are given to solve the problem of deaths of children.

2

Review of Literature and Research Methodology

2.1. INTRODUCTION

Malnutrition is a worldwide problem. Over millions of people are starving and underfed in the whole world due to lack of food, lack of knowledge and lack of facilities. There are several researches which have demonstrated the relationship of nutrition status to health, vigor and achievements. In developing countries like India, malnutrition is one of the biggest obstacles to human progress and to socio-economic development. The effects become serious depending upon the degree of malnutrition. It is dangerous for infants and children who need adequate quantity as well as quality of food for their physical and mental growth and for realizing their full genetic potential. The children from various parts of Maharashtra are suffering from this problem. The selected area of present study is also one of them.

2.2. AREA UNDER STUDY

Amravati district is situated in Maharashtra. It is 150 Kms from Nagpur, the second capital of Maharashtra. The Amravati district covers 12.212 sq. kms *i.e.,* 3.96 percent of the total area of Maharashtra state which covers 3,07,713 sq. kms of the land. From the administrative point of view, this district is divided into 14 talukas, namely Amravati, Bhatkuli, Nandgaon Khandeshwar, Achalpur, Chandur Bazar, Morshi, Warud, Chandur Railway, Tiwasa, Daryapur, Anjangaon, Dhamangaon Railway, Dharni and Chikhaldara. The last two *i.e.,* Dharni and Chikhaldara are jointly known as Melghat which is our actual area of study and will be discussed in later sections.

As per the 1991 census, the Amravati district includes 11 cities and 1681 villages which are densely populated and 315 scarcely populated villages. The Government of Maharashtra has declared the Amravati city as the Regional Headquarter.

To the north of this district, lies the Satpuda Ranges which consists of Warud, Morshi, Chandur Bazar, Achalpur, Chikhaldara and Dharni. Most of the parts of Dhamangaon, Chikhaldara and Dharni are hilly and have *ghats,* forest area. Wardha River flows to the eastern side of this district and it forms the border of Nagpur and Amravati district. It flows through Warud, Morshi, Tiwasa and Dhamangaon Railway talukas. The remaining part of this district is almost plains.

The landed area of Amravati district is made up of volcanic lava and is black in colour. This type of land is known as black cotton soil. The river *Purna is the main river of this district. This river arises from the Satpuda ranges near Bhaisdehi in* Madhya Pradesh and flows from north to south from the mid part of this district. It further flows into Jalgaon district and joins the river *Tapi. Similarly, the River Pedhi. Chandrabhaga, Shahanoor and Borda, which are the tributories of Purna, also flows through this district.*

In Amravati district, there is 3577 sq. kms. of forest area which is 29.29 percent of the total land. Most of the forest area lies in the north-western part of this district *i.e.,* Morshi, Chikhaldara and Dharni talukas. In these forests, *teak, bamboo, Chandan, Tendu-* leaves and gum, etc. are produced.

The weather of this district is hot and dry. Here, the temperature starts falling from October and reaches to its lowest in December, when it is quite cold. It starts rising from February and until mid summer it becomes extremely hot. The monsoon in this district starts in June and it rains upto October.

2.3. POPULATION

According to the just published census report of 2001, the total population of Amravati district is 26.06.063 whereas it was 22.00.000 in the year 1991 as per the census record of 1991. Thus, the population has increased by 18.45 percent since 1991. In this district, according to the 2001 census report, the density of the population is 213 persons per sq. kms as compared to 314 persons per sq. km in Maharashtra. This shows that Amravati district has less density of population as compared to Maharashtra. Also, the district has scarcely populated villages with population density of 142 persons per sq. km. whereas in the cities the density is 5442 person per sq. km. Amongst the Tehsils in Amravati district, the highest density is in Anjangaon Surji which is 17.889 persons per sq. km. The other places like Amravati, Chandur Bazar, Daryapur and Achalpur are also densely populated with approximately 6000 to 10000 persons per sq. km. Out of the total population of Amravati district, the percentage of population in villages is 65.49 percent and 34.51 percent population in cities. The most densely populated city is the head quarter *i.e.,* Amravati with 61.08 percent of the total population and the most scarcely populated is Chikhaldara with 0.52 percent of the total population.

According to the census report of 2001, there are 940 women per every 1000 men whereas the proportion of state is 922 women per 1000 men. Also, this proportion of women and men in the cities and villages are 936 and 942 per 1000, respectively.

The literacy rate of women and men are high as compared to the literacy rate of state as revealed by the 2001 census. Out of the total population of Amravati district 83 percent are literate as compared to 77 percent in Maharashtra. From the total literate population in Amravati 89 percent are men as compared to 86 percent in Maharashtra and 76 percent are women as compared to 68 percent in Maharashtra.

2.4. MELGHAT

Melghat is situated in the southern off shoot of Satpuda ranges and north eastern Maharashtra in Amravati district. It is constituted by incorporating two Tehsils of

Amravati district namely Dharni and Chikhaldara. The term Melghat (Mel - Ghat) means meeting of hills and the people of this area are known as Melghatis. The land area of Dharni and Chikhaldara is 1463 sq. kms and 2508 sq. kms, respectively and thus, the total area of Melghat is 3971 sq. kms.. The total number of villages in Melghat region is 300, out of which 153 are in Dharni and 197 in Chikhaldara. Out of these 300 villages, 33 are not having any population. The human population of Dharni and Chikhaldara is 147000 and 96000 persons respectively, as per the report of 2001 census. Therefore, the total population of Melghat is 243 thousand persons. As far as urban and rural population is concerned, the total population of Dharni is rural whereas 91000 of Chikhaldara are rural. Hence, only 5000 persons of Melghat are living in urban area and that too in Chikhaldara. Thus, almost whole population of Melghat is rural except 5000 of Chikhaldara. Most of the population of Melghat area is scheduled tribe which includes Korkus, Gonds and Nihals mainly. The remaining population is that of Balai, Gawalan, Gaolies and others.

Melghat is the green treasure of Maharashtra. Here, a variety of flora and fauna are available. As per the record of 1998-99, the percentage of forest area in the Dharni and Chikhaldara were 12 percent and 87 percent respectively. Day by day, the forests are reducing due to uncontrolled cutting of trees. The nature of forests over the major area of Melghat is of dry deciduous type. Teak (Sagwan) is the most common and dominant tree throughout this area. The other kind of trees are also available in this forest *e.g.*, Moin, Aola, Ghoti, Tiwas, Amaltas, Tendu, Sajad, Haldu, Gum and Dudhi, etc.. Botany's researchers have identified more than 150 plant species. Some of them are rare medicinal plants, and the uses as well as information regarding such plants are known only to the local tribal residents of the region.

The people of this region are less literate, backward and away from modem scientific developments. Thus, the economy of this region is very poor. Here, the main occupation is agriculture. The crops like wheat, rice, jowar, pulse, vegetable, fruits, cotton, etc. are produced in small amount by farmers of this region. Also, the people of Melghat do the animal raring, collection of forest products, production of milk, etc. for their livelihood.

The *korkus* are chiefly found in Melghat Tehsil of Amravati district. The *korkus* consider themselves as Hindus and worship Hindu God. Also, many of them have converted to Christianity for different reasons. The *korkus* of Melghat are today spending their life, more or less, like other ruralites and do not show much distinctive characteristics typical of their forefathers. They have their own tradition and culture which are reasonably different from those of other non tribals.

2.4.1. Study on Tribes Status

There are about 250 tribal communities in India with a population of about 8 percent of the country. Out of the total population of tribes, 80 percent are concentrated in central belt of India (Fernandes, 1993). Melghat is one of the parts of that area. The tribal society is very near to the nature. Due to their geographical remoteness, many tribal are socially and economically backward. There is illiteracy, malnourishment and ignorance in the tribal population. Presently, the tribal are not into the main stream of our country. Many efforts have been made for the tribal development since independence.The socio-economic status is a very important aspect which is being employed frequently in the study of such matters particularly nutritional status. The poor economic condition of the tribal society is a great hindrance to education. Almost all the tribes do not have sufficient food to maintain their family for the whole year. Education, therefore, is a luxury to them which they can hardly afford. Each school going child in a tribal family is an economic unit and contributes to the income of the family. According to the present system of education, any economic benefit, a tribal child can bring to his family will be only after ten or fifteen years of education. The parents have neither the patience nor the foresight to wait for such a long period. More allocation of funds and opening of schools do not go far, in providing education to the tribal people. Social factors play very important role in this respect. Hence, formal education or schooling has made very little impact on tribal society. Shah and Patel (1984) reported that the educational development of the people in the tribal area is generally very low. The educational development of the females is much lower than that of males. In 62.7 percent of households, women have not obtained any formal education and in 33.2 percent households men have not obtained any formal education. The highest levels of education obtained by any member among the females, the percentage of households vary from 15.7 percent for primary education to 0.8 percent for graduation. Patel (1985) has shown that about 29 percent families have been found to be literate and 71 percent illiterate in Melghat region whereas 40.83 percent males and 15.56 percent females are literate. Awlaskar (1968) has conducted a study on education and found that education has been always the source of wealth and power as well as social and economic status in India.

2.4.2. Economic Status

As economic survey of the tribal labour reveals that migration of main tribal families occur due to work in big plants away from their villages. It has also been reported that the tribals are preferred over other labours because of their larger output of work and that too at lower wages (see Thakur, 1986). James (1982) has suggested that the per capita income of such areas are significantly below the average national income and the incidence of poverty is significantly higher than other regions in terms of the proportion of the population below poverty line as defined by the Government.

The economic condition of the tribals in India and its consequent reaction on their social life is distinctly particular to that of any other place of inhibition *i.e.,* hill tops, slopes, dense forest or other isolated areas. Their principal professions are land cultivation and exploitation of forest products. They have been forced out of other professions because of their illiteracy, ignorance, and social backwardness. This encouraged the people of other classes to exploit them and they have been ultimately reduced to a status of merely landless labours (see Thakur, 1986).

2.4.3. Land Holding

The state of agriculture in the tribal area is comparatively very backward and pitiable. Small land holdings are continuously encouraged upon all sides. Poor quality of the soil and primitive methods of cultivation are responsible for low agricultural yields. These agricultural yields are not adequate to sustain people throughout the year. Ultimately, they start consuming locally available fruits, roots and wild vegetables to supplement their insufficient food. The tribals raise only food crops in many cases for domestic and local consumption (see Thakur, 1986).

The tribals depend on agriculture for four months and on forest for eight months. The children in the age group of 4 to 6 years have been found to be helping their parents in the collection of forest products. In this situation, the parents do not wish to spare their children or labour power and allow them to attend school.

2.4.4. Food Habits

The tribals of India are mostly non-vegetarian though they do not get it daily. The tribal people generally take two meals in a day. One in the morning before going to work and another in the evening after returning. The tribal's diet mainly consists of jowar, rice and toor-dal. Sometimes, they eat only jowar roti with chutney. Some families prepare "Ghata" from coarsely grounded jowar. This is their traditional recipe. Most of the time, they eat boiled rice. If they prepare rice and dal then they do not prepare jowar roties on that day. Food is cooked by usual methods of cooking like roasting, boiling, etc.. Also they do not have knowledge of preparation of various dishes and so their diet is stereo-typed. Their diet also lacks oil and milk. They only prepare puri and halwa for their festivals (Singh, 1993).

2.5. MALNUTRITION

For maintaining good health and physical efficiency, the diet should provide adequate amounts of all nutrients.

For a balanced diet, it is essential to know the daily requirements of different nutrients. In other words, a balanced diet may be defined as, one which contains the various groups of foodstuffs such as energy yielding foods, body building foods and protective foods in the correct proportion, so that an individual is assured of obtaining the minimum requirements of all the nutrients. The components of a balanced diet will differ according to age, sex, physical activities, economic status and the physiological state *viz*; pregnancy, lactation, etc..

A balanced diet contains foods such as milk, eggs, meat, fish and fruits, cereals, pulses, nuts and fats, green leafy vegetables, other vegetables, roots and tubers, sugar and jaggery, etc.. The amount of intake of these things will vary according to age, sex, physical activity, economic status and the physiological state. But when people fail to consume such balanced diet due to different reasons such as lack of knowledge or economic condition, etc. they are at a risk of becoming malnourished (Swaminathan, 1985). A proper definition of malnutrition has been defined by World Health Organization (WHO), Geneva as "The term is used to refer to a number of diseases, each with a specific cause related to one or more nutrients (for example, protein, iodine or calcium) and each characterised by cellular imbalance between the supply of nutrients and energy on the one hand, and the body's demand for them to ensure growth, maintenance and specific functions, on the other". More information about malnutrition, its different forms, efficiency caused by it, remedies, etc. can be downloaded from *hup : / / wmw.who.ch / /.* the website of W.H.O..

There are various types of diseases and infections that can be caused due to malnutrition (see Scrimshaw *et al.*,

1968). The deficiency of different nutritional requirements causes different diseases, and many of them can even be fatal in some cases. A few diseases and their causes are discussed below:

1) Protein deficiency in infants, probably modified by vitamin and mineral deficiencies is now considered as one of the most important world health problems. It is known as Kwashiorkor, Infantile pellagra, multiple deficiency syndrome, etc. in various parts of the world and is characterised chiefly by odema, liver dysfunction, emaciation and various skin changes. It is most severe in the post weaning period when satisfactory foods are not available to replace breast milk (see Brock *et al.*, 1952) and Blank, 1996).

2) The symptoms of vitamin A deficiency are principally: (a) night blindness related to the function in the visual cycle, (b) failure of bone growth, thus causing paralysis, and (c) metamorphosis of the normal secreting epithelium of the nose, throat, urogenital tract, eye, etc. into a dry squamous type epithelium.

3) Vitamin D is formed in the skin. Its deficiency causes continuous excretion of calcium, thus resulting in softening of bones. Due to this, some commonly occurring symptoms are seen, such as malformed bowed legs, muscle lone is poor and enlarged and sagging abdomen is seen and in many cases even racket develops.

4) Vitamin E deficiency causes dry and scaly skin conditions.

5) Vitamin K deficiency occur in human beings under two cases: (a) in liver diseases. (b) in new born infants. Large number of infants die of hemorrhage shortly after birth due to trauma suffered at birth. Apparently, in infants the level of vitamin K is not sufficient until the gastro intestinal flora becomes established.

6) Vitamin C deficiency causes the scurvy disease in children. It is also administered to children when they catch cough and common cold.

7) The recent report has shown that the deficiency of vitamin B_6 develops in infants due to feeding of certain prepared formula (Molony and Parwelle, 1954) and Vilter, 1953).

8) Calcium deficiency causes Rickets and osteomalacia. Both are essentially diseases of childhood, pregnancy and lactation when calcium requirements are high.

9) The iron deficiency is related to menstrual blood losses and fetus formation in adult women. Iron deficiency, *i.e.,* Anemia is common in women and children.

10) A deficiency of thiamine produces the disease beriberi in children and in some extreme cases it even causes chastek paralysis.

Malnutrition in Children

For the healthy growth and healthy development of the body of a child, food plays an important role. The health of children is of great concern to developing countries like India as they are our future citizens. One of the W.H.O.

report states that more than 50 percent children of the age of upto 5 years die every year directly or indirectly due to nutritional deficiencies.

Childhood is perhaps the most critical and vulnerable period. This is the time when the child needs acceptance, love and nutrients to nourish his body and stimulate his mind. In large areas of the world today, malnutrition especially among young children *i.e.,* in the age-group of 0-5 years is one of the most important public health problems (see http:// www.who.ch//). Mortality and morbidity level are high in malnourished children and even common infections or diseases can often become catastrophic (see W.H.O, 1963). Better child feeding practices probably can make important contributions to the reduction of mortality rate for protection against the child malnutrition. Quantifications of malnutrition therefore become important. This is possible through clinical examinations and also through assessment of the status of growth subject to the condition that there is a good agreement between nutritional status and body measure.

Krishnamachari and Rao (1964) have shown that about 30 percent of the children below the age of 5 years have one or more sign of nutritional deficiency. Nearly 60 percent of children had moderate to severe degree of malnutrition on the basis of weight deficit for age. Ali (1987) has conducted a study on Lanjia saora tribes and his study revealed that the cases of malnutrition were high among the children. The women were not given a reasonable share of food as compared to the men and such intra-household food distribution system has been probably responsible for continuing the cycle of malnutrition among the children.

A recent report of integrated child welfare services shows that on a country-wide basis the prevalence of severe grades of malnutrition among pre-school going children vary from 1 percent to 15 percent among tribal groups (Shrikanta and Vishwesara, 1982). Pingle's (1991) study area was on Koya tribal children in Mailgram and it shows that almost all pre-school children become anemic by September and show a moderate to severe grade of malnutrition. Jha *et al.* (1988) revealed that the average per capita income of the Baigas is very low. About three-fourth of the income from non-agricultural sources come from labour activities organized by the government. Mathur (1987) has conducted his study on children of 0-5 years of age-group. A total of 1.464 children were studied and examined clinically. About 36 percent of the children under five in the developing countries excluding China, out of 150 million who were studied, are malnourished *i.e.,* they are under-weight, about 39 percent of 163 million are stunted and 8 percent are wasted. One in six malnourished children is severely malnourished (see Carlson and Wardlaw, 1990).

Najtilka *et al.* (1996) has carried out his study to find out health problems of 1-5 years of children. It has been seen that the children of illiterate and poor tribals had higher prevalence of the disease than those of literate tribal mothers. The boys were affected more than girls. Vaidya and Taneja (1996) have studied the nutritional status of 706 pre-school children of 0-6 year's age-group belonging to 430 Bhil tribal families of Jhabua district in Madhya Pradesh. Information about family size was collected by interviews. Nutritional status was assessed through Anthropometric and clinical examination of all the children. The study shows moderate and severe malnutrition. A comprehensive survey was carried out by

Rao *et al.* (1966) to assess the nutritional status of 3115 pre-school children in rural area near Hyderabad city. The result indicates that the children examined have one or more signs of nutritional deficiency (see also Rao *et al.*, 1978; 1987; 1996).

2.6. Some Basic Concepts in Demography

Demography is an ever growing subject and as in the case of other subjects, in this subject some basic concepts are used *e.g.,* demographic data is technically known as demographic events. Some commonly used concepts include still-birth, family size, live-birth, child-death and marriage, etc.. Here, it is essential that some of the required basic concepts must be properly defined for correct study of present research work. Without clearly defining these terms, there can be some misunderstandings and difficulties in analysis. It is very essential that these concepts should be carefully and uniformly used.

Live Births

Live birth is the beginning of life and influences population. Live birth is the complete expulsion or extraction from the mother of a product of conception irrespective of the duration of pregnancy, which after such separation breathes or shows any other evidence of life such as beating of heart, pulsation of umbilical cord has been cut or the placenta is attached, each product of such birth is considered live birth. Live birth is very important both in the growth of population and social life. In the growth of population it is important because boy of today becomes father of tomorrow and a girl of today will tomorrow be a mother. Socially live birth becomes important because boy and girl become shareholders in property.

Still Birth

Demographers define birth by including both live birth and still birth. Live birth as defined above is of-course somewhat simpler in counting because in it, all babies are counted who take birth. But problem arises in the case of still births. In still birth, all those children are included who did not come out of the womb of the mother, but the woman remained pregnant for 28 weeks. The United Nations Organization has defined it as, "a still birth is a foetal death occurring late in the gestation occurring, late is usually defined as after 28 completed weeks of gestation", Gestation being understood as period from conception to birth.

Foetal Death

The United Nations Organization has defined foetal death as, "Foetal death is a death prior to the complete expulsion or extraction from its mother of a product of conception irrespective of the duration of pregnancy, the death is indicated by the fact that after extraction the foetus does not breath or show any other evidence of life".

Infant and Child Deaths

There are main deaths due to social or other causes within a period of six years from the birth of the child. The study of child death is very important for the Demographers. As the child grows, with that the probability of death becomes less. Deaths which occur within a period of one year from the birth of a child are known as infant deaths, whereas those deaths which take place between a period of one to six years, are known as child deaths.

2.7. OBJECTIVES

The following objectives have been considered before making the present study:

1) To study the problem of malnutrition in Melghat *i.e.,* Dharni and Chikhaldara taluka.
2) To study the last three years data of malnutrition and deaths of children through statistical analysis.
3) To study the economical factors of the families.
4) To fit a mathematical model for economical factors.
5) To study a Demographical factors of malnutrition.
6) To fit a mathematical model for Demographic variables.

2.8. HYPOTHESIS

The following hypothesis are to be tested:

1) Number of males and females shall be nearly equal over the whole population.
2) Male population will be more than females at younger age (*i.e.,* less than 20 years) and females will be more than males from the age of 20 years and onwards due to job migration.

3) Internal migration especially long distance movements shall be at minimum. Marriage migration shall be the only way of territorial mobility that too upto a short distance.
4) The standard of education will be very low.
5) The knowledge of family planning and the means of adopting it shall be low.
6) The fertility rate is expected to be high.
7) Mortality rates are expected to be high.
8) Family income should be very low.

2.9. RESEARCH METHODOLOGY

The sampling plan is essential as it affects the cost of the study and the time taken to complete the data collection. The number of subjects needed for any survey or study depends on the questions being asked, the critical region size and the statistical accuracy (power) desired. Road in Melghat (Source-Nayak, 2012).

A well structured questionnaire was prepared considering the general information as well as the economical and demographical factors. This questionnaire has been filled by asking questions to the respondents. Out of 300 villages of Melghat, 10 villages have been selected randomly. The names of the villages are shown in Table 2.1. A list of households on the basis of census of household number has been obtained from the Patwari of the village. The unit of enquiry *i.e.,* household meant all members in a house, who had a common kitchen (chullah) and who lived under one roof. From each village, households are randomly selected in proportion to the total

Table 2.1: Details of Villages with number of respondents

Name	***Frequency***	***Percent***
Alladoh	20	6.6
Bahavi	18	6.0
Bibamal	31	10.3
Bihali	32	10.7
Dhomna	25	8.3
Gavlandoh	23	7.7
Ghatang	12	4.0
Kohana	13	4.3
Kusumkot	18	6.0
Motha	17	5.7
Pattharpur	30	10.0
Semadoh	32	10.7
Zilpi	29	9.7
Total	300	100

households of the village subject to the condition that the total samples must be 300. A sample of size 300 tribal women has also been considered by Tekhre (1989), while evaluating the impact of the family welfare program on tribal women of Tamian development block of Chindwara district of Madhya Pradesh. In three villages, namely Ghatang, Motha and Kusumkot, it has been very difficult to get the decided number of respondents. In such situation the respondents of nearest village had been contacted and their response has been taken. These cases are considered as respondent of the original village (see Table 2.2).

From each village a married male or female has been questioned to get the required details of the questionnaire by direct questioning. A simple Marathi version of questionnaire has been used for respondents. In addition to the method of direct interview, the method of schedule

Table 2.2: The details of sampling

Sl.no.	*Particulars*	*Number*
1.	Decided number of sample data	300
2.	Decided number of villages	10
3.	Actual contacted number of respondents	681
4.	Number of respondents not replied	381
5.	Final number of respondents	300
6.	Number of villages contacted to get complete data	13
7.	Additional neighboring villages	03

and observation are adopted to seek additional information on economic status, family planning and various other aspects. The help of local person was essential because the language of respondents *i.e.*, 'korku' was difficult and so it made conversation very difficult. The respondents were told the purpose of the survey, as to learn about the reasons of deaths of children in this region. The personal interview took about 30 minutes to complete the questionnaire due to the less educational qualifications of the respondents. Since, the whole day the adult male or female of a village go to their work either in a field or far- away place, and non -availability of electric light in night, had made this task difficult.

Before the primary data collection by direct questioning a secondary data from the district health office has been collected and analysed so as to be familiar and get some idea of the problem and the area under study. The so collected data has been analysed and the conclusions based on these have been presented in the chapters later on. The tables to show the summarized data have been prepared considering the requirement of that data and to present in the form of frequency distribution. The computational work has been performed directly using the SPSS software with the help of original values of observations. It is important to note here that, if the calculations would have been performed using traditional statistical methods on the tables then that may minutely differ from our results obtained using SPSS software, though the conclusions will be same.

Road in Melghat (*Source* – Nayak, 2012)

Road in Melghat (*Source* – Nayak, 2012)

3

Analysis of District Health Office Data

3.1. INTRODUCTION

This chapter is a pilot work before starting the analysis of the data, collected by the author herself. The data used here is a secondary data gathered by Amravati District Health Office, Amravati. This office is a branch of Zilla Parishad, Amravati and functions under the collector, Amravati. This office also tabulates the data collected by Integrated Child Development Scheme, Amravati and submits to higher authorities. This is totally a government organization. This office is having several schemes to remove the problem of deaths of children in Melghat region. Some of such health schemes are as follows:

(1) Area Volunteers Scheme

Under this scheme, the local people are trained and appointed as area workers on a honorarium of Rs. 300 - per month to establish a co-ordination between the tribal society and the health machinery. One or two volunteers in each village and around 700 total volunteers are appointed in the period, between the months of May to October. These volunteers are expected to go everyday from door to door and find out the number of ill children as well as treat them. They also explain the tribals in their language about health and nutrition.

(2) Honorary Medical Officers Scheme

To make the medical facilities easily available to the villagers, 22 mobile medical practitioner's teams work in this region in the period of between the months from May to December. These mobile teams are given vehicles with enough stock of medicines and they are expected to visit the villages again and again. They are expected to find out the ill and malnourished children, pregnant women and lactating mothers and treat as well as give them necessary medicines. With every mobile team there is a doctor appointed on a honorarium of Rs. 4000/- per month.

(3) Financial Support Scheme for Pregnant Mothers

Tribal families are very poor and men as well as women of every family work. The women have to work hard for earning their living even during pregnancy. Because of this, they give birth to underweight children or sometimes premature babies. In order to avoid this and allow them to take complete rest and nutritious foods, under this scheme, the women in their 7th to 9th months of pregnancy are paid Rs. 200/- per month by government. Also, after their delivery, once again they are given Rs. 200/-. Thus a total of Rs. 800/- are provided to them as financial support.

(4) Mid-wife's Refresher Sitting Scheme

It is expected that the delivery of a baby will be handled by a mid-wife in the region. For safe deliver and in the same way to avoid the deaths of mothers as well as the new born, all the trained and untrained mid-wives of this region are given sittings. In these sittings, they are taught to take care of the pregnant women, to make a safe delivery, to take care of the new born, to take care of the babies born under weight, etc.. Such type of meetings are arranged every month and for attending this, the mid-wives are paid allowances as well as T.A. and D.A.

(5) Special Facilities for Serious Cases

In the Melghat region, it has been a common phenomena that the parents of even very seriously malnourished children avoid to visit the hospital or take the proper care of their children just because of the loss of their daily wages. To motivate them to take proper care, the malnourished children of grade 3 and grade 4, who are admitted in the primary health centers or hospitals and their relatives coming with them, are provided free meals, twice a day with a daily compen-sation of Rs. 40/- until a child is admit in the health centre hospital.

(6) Boco Box Facility

To save the underweight new born or premature babies of dying from Hypothermia and Hypoglycemia, thermocol boxes called as Boco boxes have been distributed to the mid-wives, nurses and also to Anganwadi centres. In these boxes, the underweight new born and premature babies are kept and taken care of.

(7) Other Schemes

A number of other facilities have also been provided to take care of the children in the proper ways. The hospitals in Melghat area have been provided with Intensive Care Unit. Also, the primary health centers have been provided with warm rooms for the same purpose. The visits of child specialists and Gynecologists have also been arranged in the hospitals.

3.2. METHOD FOR GRADING THE MALNOURISHED CHILDREN

A number of schemes explained above are being run by government at different levels in the Melghat region. Even then a number of children are malnourished and dying due to this. To know the implementation of schemes, benefits drawn from it and the different categories of malnutrition of children, government have a data collection system too. They are collecting the information regarding total deaths of children, deaths in the different age group and the number of malnourished children of various grades. This helps the health authorities to treat and take care of the children accordingly and properly. The criteria of deciding these grades have been provided by UNICEF.

The children in the age group of 0-5 years are graded for their stages of malnourishment. These grades decide the seriousness of their malnourishment. Earlier these grades were decided by measuring the circumference of their arms. The arm circumference was measured using a special type of strip which was prepared and provided by UNICEF. This strip was divided in three colours *i.e.*,

12.5 cms of red then 1 cm yellow and remaining green. One strip was used for one child *i.e.,* for every child a separate strip is used and the same strip was used throughout the childhood. The continuous marking of the arm circumference was done on the strip which helped in assessing the growth. The three colours were the indication of very serious, serious and normal state of malnourishment (see Vijayraghavan and Sastry, 1976).

Later on, it was found that the strip criteria lacked in accuracy, and so before a couple of years it was rejected. A new criterion was introduced in which the grading of malnutrition is being done according to the weight of the children. The age and weight both are continuous variables. It is very natural, as the child grows and age increases, it results in the increase in weight too. If the weight of children does not increase in harmony with the age then there is imbalance in the development of the child and it becomes a state of malnutrition. This state has been divided in five grades. The graph of weights according to their ages, which decides the five grades of malnutrition, has been distributed by UNICEF and the same is given as graph G3.1.

It can be seen from the graph G 3.1 that if a baby is born more than 2.9 kgs of weight then it is considered as a normal child. If the weight is between 2.5 to 2.9 kgs then it is considered as malnourished in grade 1. If the weight of the baby at birth lies between 2.0 to 2.5 kgs then it is malnourished in grade 2, between 1.6 to 2.0 kgs in grade 3 and below 1.6 kgs then the child is in grade 4. Moreover, the children in grade 4 and grade 3 of malnutrition are considered as seriously malnourished.

The constant trend of weight growth is shown for each grade upto 5 years of age in the graph. A very rapid growth

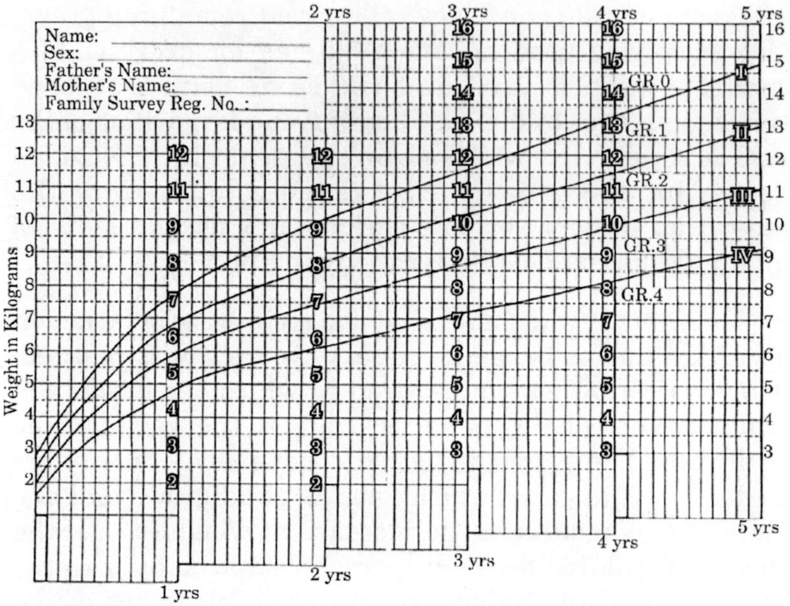

Graph G. 3.1: Growth Chart - From Birth to Age 5

is shown during the infant age period, *i.e.,* zero to one year of age. At one year of age if the child is above 7.8 kgs of weight, it is considered as normal. It is considered in the grade 1 of malnutrition if the weight is between 6.9 to 7.8 kgs. Also, a child is malnourished of grade 2, grade 3 and grade 4 if the weight lies between 6.0 to 6.9 kgs, between 4.9 to 6.0 kgs and below 4.9 kgs, respectively.

Similarly, the different grades of malnutrition of children can be obtained upto the age of 5 years on the basis of age and weight with the help of graph G3.1. The children reaching at the exact 5 years of age, if it weighs more than 14.7 kg, such children are considered as normal and less than 9.2 kgs as grade 4 of malnutrition. Whereas, weighing between 12.9 kgs to 14.7, between

11 to 12.9 kgs and 9.2 to 11 kgs arc considered as grade 1, grade 2 and grade 3, respectively.

3.3. HYPOTHESIS ASSUMED FOR TESTING

Sometimes the circumstances may be such that the children might be more malnourished and or dying due to the effect of seasons. In other words, the deaths or malnourishment may be occurring in a particular season due to climatic change or weather *i.e.*, in a particular month. Also, the questions may arise, whether the number of cases in different grades of malnutrition are equally distributed and or, are the deaths happening equally in all age - groups?

To get the answers of such doubts following hypothesis are assumed

i) H_{01}: There is no significant effect of different seasons on malnutrition.

ii) H_{02}: There is no significant difference in the number of cases in the different grades of malnutrition.

iii) H_{03}: There is no significant effect of different seasons on the number of deaths due to malnutrition.

iv) H_{04}: There is no significant difference in different age-groups due to malnutrition deaths.

3.4. ANALYSIS OF DATA

In this section, the data obtained from Amravati district health office has been analyzed. The data is obtained, is from January 1999 to December 2001 *i.e.,* of the last three years. Table 3.1 provides the data of number of

Table 3.1: Total (T) number of children in the age-group of 0-6 years and number of children each grade of malnutrition from January 1999 to December 2001

Months	*T. Child*	*Grade 0*	*Grade 1*	*Grade 2*	*Grade 3*	*Grade 4*
Jan-99	39514	13057	15047	10664	653	93
Feb-99	39732	13233	15201	10489	733	76
Mar-99	40103	13667	15225	10469	664	78
Apr-99	39304	12823	14454	11006	931	90
May-99	41430	13803	15209	11236	1024	158
Jun-99	40864	12377	15031	12194	1102	160
Jul-99	42011	12752	16322	11793	993	151
Aug-99	41265	13331	15192	11658	941	143
Sep-99	42111	14547	14969	11599	875	121
Oct-99	45408	13064	15555	15894	801	94
Nov-99	41682	14140	15775	11008	688	71
Dec-99	42146	15457	15770	10231	629	59
Jan-00	42401	15632	15798	10302	614	55
Feb-00	42603	15551	16170	10103	723	56
Mar-00	42678	15593	16293	10213	528	51
Apr-00	38738	11609	16198	10306	567	58
May-00	43533	15014	16344	11357	731	87
Jun-00	42704	14263	15377	11811	1114	139
Jul-00	42901	14646	15035	11888	1170	162
Aug-00	42791	14275	15108	11942	1259	207
Sep-00	43060	14291	15364	12171	1067	167
Oct-00	43091	14735	14840	12344	1020	152
Nov-00	40376	13948	14196	11263	842	127
Dec-00	40459	13769	14865	10946	786	93
Jan-01	42012	14972	15352	10907	712	69
Feb-01	44120	16886	15430	11094	649	61
Mar-01	42327	14730	15848	11041	645	63
Apr-01	42679	15113	15500	11230	754	82
May-01	40799	14194	13148	11672	1527	258
Jun-01	41120	12911	15106	11835	1123	145

Table 3.1: (*Contd...*)

Table 3.1: (*Contd...*)

Months	*T. Child*	*Grade 0*	*Grade 1*	*Grade 2*	*Grade 3*	*Grade 4*
Jul-01	41185	13074	15042	11843	1059	167
Aug-01	41712	13263	14948	12211	1103	187
Sep-01	41818	13362	15016	12220	1022	198
Oct-01	41182	13282	15052	11758	929	161
Nov-01	42114	14409	15171	11624	776	134
Dec-01	42033	14098	15611	11552	662	110

children in each grade from zero to four of malnutrition. This table also gives the total number of children in the age group of 0-6 years from January 1999 to December 2001. Similarly, the official data regarding deaths are given in Table 3.6. This table presents the total percentage of still births and deaths of children in the age groups of 0-1, 1-3 and 3-6. The total number of deaths and still births are also given in Table 3.5. These data are from January 1999 to December 2001.

3.4.1 Analysis of Various Grades

The total number of children in the age group of 0 to 6 years in Melghat region from Jan. 1999 to Dec. 2001 is given in the Table 3.1. Also, this table gives the normal children *i.e.,* grade zero, grade 1, grade 2, grade 3 and grade 4 malnourished children in the age group of 0-6 years from January 1999 to December 2001. The percentage of malnourished children of grade 0 *i.e.* normal, grade 1, grade 2, grade 3 and grade 4 have been calculated and presented in Table 3.2. From this table it can be observed that the percentage of normal children is almost everywhere more than thirty except for the month of October 1999 and April 2000. Thus, 28.77 which is

Table 3.2: Percentage of children in different grades of malnutrition

Months	*Grade 0*	*Grade 1*	*Grade 2*	*Grade 3*	*Grade 4*
Jan-99	33.0440	38.0802	26.9879	1.6526	0.2354
Feb-99	33.3056	38.2588	26.3994	1.8449	0.1913
Mar-99	34.0797	37.9647	26.1053	1.6557	0.1945
Apr-99	32.6252	36.7749	28.0022	2.3687	0.2290
May-99	33.3164	36.7101	27.1204	2.4716	0.3814
Jun-99	30.2883	36.7830	29.8404	2.6968	0.3915
Jul-99	30.3540	38.8517	28.0712	2.3637	0.3594
Aug-99	32.3058	36.8157	28.2515	2.2804	0.3465
Sep-99	34.5444	35.5465	27.5439	2.0778	0.2873
Oct-99	28.7703	34.2561	35.0026	1.7640	0.2070
Nov-99	33.9235	37.8461	26.4095	1.6506	0.1703
Dec-99	36.6749	37.4175	24.2751	1.4924	0.1400
Jan-00	36.8671	37.2586	24.2966	1.4481	0.1297
Feb-00	36.5021	37.9551	23.7143	1.6971	0.1314
Mar-00	36.5364	38.1766	23.9304	1.2372	0.1195
Apr-00	29.9680	41.8142	26.6044	1.4637	0.1497
May-00	34.4888	37.5439	26.0883	1.6792	0.1998
Jun-00	33.3997	36.0083	27.6578	2.6087	0.3255
Jul-00	34.1391	35.0458	27.7103	2.7272	0.3776
Aug-00	33.3598	35.3065	27.9077	2.9422	0.4837
Sep-00	33.1886	35.6804	28.2652	2.4779	0.3878
Oct-00	34.1951	34.4387	28.6464	2.3671	0.3527
Nov-00	34.5453	35.1595	27.8953	2.0854	0.3145
Dec-00	34.0320	36.7409	27.0545	1.9427	0.2299
Jan-01	35.6374	36.5419	25.9616	1.6948	0.1642
Feb-01	38.2729	34.9728	25.1451	1.4710	0.1383
Mar-01	34.8005	37.4418	26.0850	1.5239	0.1488
Apr-01	35.4109	36.3176	26.3127	1.7667	0.1921
May-01	34.7901	32.2263	28.6085	3.7427	0.6324
Jun-01	31.3983	36.7364	28.7816	2.7310	0.3526
Jul-01	31.7446	36.5230	28.7556	2.5713	0.4055
Aug-01	31.7966	35.8362	29.2745	2.6443	0.4483
Sep-01	31.9527	35.9080	29.2219	2.4439	0.4735
Oct-01	32.2520	36.5499	28.5513	2.2558	0.3909
Nov-01	34.2143	36.0237	27.6013	1.8426	0.3182
Dec-01	33.5403	37.1399	27.4832	1.5750	0.2617

minimum percentage of normal children was in October 1999 and the maximum percentage *i.e.*, 38.27 in February 2001. Moreover, the percentage of normal children is more or less equal and lies between 28 to 37.

For grade 1 type of malnutrition in Table 3.2, the minimum percentage is 32.22 in May 2001 and maximum *i.e.,* 41.81 in April 2000. The minimum percentage of grade 2 malnourished children is 23.71 in Feb. 2000 and maximum 35.00 in October 1999. For grade 3 and grade 4, the minimum percentage *i.e.,* 1.23 and 0.11, respectively are in March 2000 and maximum *i.e.,* 3.74 and 0.63 respectively in May 2001. Table 3.2 also reveals the fact that the percentage of malnourished children in all the grades are nearly equal during all the three years and does not show any reduction in number of malnourished children. Hence, it is clear that there is no improvement in the status of different grades of malnourished children due to the schemes run by government.

To find the trend of total children, let an analytical expression *i.e.,* the parametric functional relationship between total child population (Y) and month (X) has the following relationship,

$$y_i = \beta_0 + \beta_1 + x_i + \epsilon_i; \; i=1, 2,..., 36$$

Where ε_i are identically independently distributed as $N(0,\sigma^2)$ and σ^2 is unknown. For this data, the least square fitted model *i.e.,* the line of best fit is

$$v = 41223.7 - 29.9609x$$

with $R^2 = 0.053$ where R^2 is residual sum of squares. This is the best fitted model. The next choice may be an exponential but that has higher value of R^2.

To test the null hypothesis H_{01} and H_{02}, set in the previous section 3.3, Analysis of Variance (ANOVA) has been done. The data given in Table 3.1 is a two way classified data with 3 observations per cell (month). After performing the intermediate calculations, the final ANOVA table for seasons and grades are given in Table 3.3. From this table, it is clear that F calculated for interaction between seasons and different grades is more than F tabulated at 5% level of significance. Therefore, there is significance of interaction effect. The calculated value of F for seasons is less than F tabulated value at 5% level of significance. Therefore, the null hypothesis H_{01}, is accepted *i.e.,* the seasons are not affecting the malnutrition of children. The F calculated value for grades is much more than the F tabulated at 5% level of significance. Thus, the null hypothesis H_{02}, is rejected *i.e.,* there is significant difference in the number of cases in the different grades of malnutrition. Now, we proceed further, to find out which pair(s) of different grades differs significantly. Here, we obtain the least significant difference at a particular level of significance. The least difference is also known as critical difference (CD) and CD, at 5% level of significance is 457.17 for error (120) degrees of freedom. The difference of means of grades have been obtained after arranging them in descending order

Table 3.3: ANOVA Table for Seasons (S) and Grades (G)

S.V.	*d.f*	*S.S.*	*MSS*	F_{cal}	F_{tab} *(0.05)*
SSS	11	3293883.578	299443.96	0.67	1.87
SSG	4	7701740997.00	1925435249.00	4334.48	2.45
SSI	44	35533066.81	807569.70	1.82	1.48
SSE	120	53305630.00			
Total	179	7793873578	444213.583		

of magnitude and are given in Table 3.4. It is clear from the table that all the differences are more than CD, *i.e.,* no number of cases are alike for different grades of malnutrition.

Table 3.4: Mean difference table for grades

Treat-ment	*Mean*	*grade 1*	*grade 2*	*grade 2*	*grade 3*	*grade 4*
grade 1	45880.2	0				
grade 0	42155.9	3724.25	0			
grade 2	34322.8	11557.33	7833.0833	0		
grade 3	2618	43262.16	39537.917	31704.8	0	
grade 4	356.91	45523.25	41799	33965.9	2261.08	0

CD. at 5% level of significance for grades = 457.173735

3.4.2. Analysis of Deaths

The health office collects the data of birth and death of the children in every month. The data of number of live-births, still births and the number of deaths, in the age group of 0 to 1, 1 to 3 and 3 to 6 are given in Table 3.5. These data are from January 1999 to December 2001. With the help of these data information, the total number of deaths in every month has been calculated from January 1999 to December 2001 and that too are presented in the same table. The percentage of deaths *i.e.*, still birth, deaths at the age of 0-1, 1-3 and 3-6 has been obtained and presented in the Table 3.6. It is clear from the table that the percentage of deaths has neither increasing nor decreasing trend but it has a zigzag type of trend. For all the four percentages, the range of spreading of values is very high. The values are distributed from 21.87 to 46.51, 25.92 to 53.73, 6.97 to 34.72 and 1.49 to 17.85 for still birth, deaths between 0 to 1, 1 to 3 and 3 to 6, respectively.

Table 3.5: Live births, still births, number of deaths of children in the age groups 0-1,1-3 and 3-6 years and total number of deaths from January 1999 to December 2001

Months	*Live births*	*Still births*	*Age group wise deaths* age 0-1	*age 1-3*	*age 3-6*	*Total deaths*
Jan-99	600	25	35	10	9	72
Feb-99	579	22	25	14	6	67
Mar-99	520	14	14	10	6	44
Apr-99	542	15	14	17	6	52
May-99	570	17	15	18	7	57
Jun-99	571	21	24	15	2	62
Jul-99	650	20	22	17	5	64
Aug-99	737	25	23	25	7	80
Sep-99	750	21	32	14	8	75
Oct-99	662	27	25	13	2	67
Nov-99	712	22	25	9	7	63
Dec-99	611	26	29	8	2	65
Jan-00	722	79	36	8	1	67
Feb-00	675	25	27	6	6	64
Mar-00	501	28	31	6	7	72
Apr-00	586	19	20	7	3	49
May-00	652	18	16	11	5	50
Jun-00	688	15	29	15	2	61
Jul-00	608	18	28	20	5	71
Aug-00	616	28	40	24	5	97
Sep-00	645	18	20	25	9	72
Oct-00	567	17	15	17	6	55
Nov-00	622	23	18	12	8	61
Dec-00	536	20	19	19	1	59
Jan-01	650	32	23	12	3	70
Feb-01	581	20	16	3	4	43
Mar-01	593	18	26	12	2	58
Apr-01	586	12	10	10	3	35
May-01	610	23	16	8	8	55
Jun-01	739	22	15	14	6	57

Table 3.5: (*Contd...*)

Table 3.5: (*Contd...*)

Months	***Live births***	***Still births***	***Age group wise deaths age 0-1***	***age 1-3***	***age 3-6***	***Total deaths***
Jul-01	603	14	19	22	9	64
Aug-01	616	20	26	29	12	87
Sep-01	527	26	22	24	8	80
Oct-01	490	14	18	16	4	52
Nov-01	503	19	15	12	10	56
Dec-01	507	15	14	16	9	54

Table 3.6: Percentage of deaths *i.e.,* still - birth, deaths at the age of 0-1, 1-3 and 3-6 years

Months	***Still births***	***age 0-1***	***age 1-3***	***age 3-6***
Jan-99	34.7222	48.6111	13.8889	2.7778
Feb-99	32.8358	37.3134	20.8955	8.9552
Mar-99	31.8182	31.8182	22.7273	13.6364
Apr-99	28.8462	26.9231	32.6923	11.5385
May-99	29.8246	26.3158	31.5789	12.2807
Jun-99	33.8710	38.7097	24.1935	3.2258
Jul-99	31.2500	34.3750	26.5625	7.8125
Aug-99	31.2500	28.7500	31.2500	8.7500
Sep-99	28.0000	42.6667	18.6667	10.6667
Oct-99	40.2985	37.3134	19.4030	2.9851
Nov-99	34.9206	39.6825	14.2857	11.1111
Dec-99	40.0000	44.6154	12.3077	3.0769
Jan-00	32.8358	53.7313	11.9403	1.4925
Feb-00	39.0625	42.1875	9.3750	9.3750
Mar-00	38.8889	43.0556	8.333	9.7222
Apr-00	38.7755	40.8163	14.2857	6.1224
May-00	36.0000	32.0000	22.0000	10.0000
Jun-00	24.5902	47.5410	24.5902	3.2787
Jul-00	25.3521	39.4366	28.1690	7.0423
Aug-00	28.8660	41.2371	24.7423	5.1546

Table 3.6: (*Contd...*)

Table 3.6: (*Contd...*)

Months	***Still births***	***age 0-1***	***age 1-3***	***age 3-6***
Sep-00	25.0000	27.7778	34.7222	12.5000
Oct-00	30.9091	27.2727	30.9091	10.9091
Nov-00	37.7049	29.5082	19.6721	13.1148
Dec-00	33.8983	32.2034	32.2034	1.6949
Jan-01	45.7143	32.8571	17.1429	4.2857
Feb-01	46.5116	37.2093	6.9767	9.3023
Mar-01	31.0345	44.8276	20.6897	3.4483
Apr-01	34.2857	28.5714	28.5714	8.5714
May-01	41.8182	29.0909	14.5455	14.5455
Jun-01	38.5965	26.3158	24.5614	10.5263
Jul-01	21.8750	29.6875	34.3750	14.0625
Aug-01	22.9885	29.8851	33.3333	13.7931
Sep-01	32.5000	27.5000	30.0000	10.0000
Oct-01	26.9231	34.6154	30.7692	7.6923
Nov-01	33.9286	26.7857	21.4286	17.8571
Dec-01	27.7778	25.9259	29.6296	16.6667

For still birth, the minimum percentage *i.e.,* 21.87 is in July 2001 and maximum 46.51 in Feb. 2001. The minimum percentage of deaths of 0 to 1 age-group is in December 2001 and maximum in January 2000. Whereas the minimum and maximum percentage of deaths for age group 1-3 are in Feb. 2001 and Sept. 2000, respectively and for age-group 3-6 are in Jan. 2000 and Nov. 2001, respectively. It can be noted that in the month of January 2000, the percentage of deaths of 0-1 age group is maximum whereas of 3-6 is minimum. Similarly, in the month of Feb. 2001, the percentage of still-birth is maximum whereas of 1-3 age-group is minimum. It seems that in a particular month if the percentage of deaths of certain age-group is decreasing then the percentage of some other age-group is increasing.

To find a mathematical function of live birth (Y), considering as dependent variable, with month (X), the best fitted model has been obtained applying the least square method. Let the model be

$$y_i = \epsilon_0 + \beta_1 x_i + \epsilon_i \; ; i=1, 2,..., 36$$

where ϵ_i***'s*** are identically independently distributed as $N(0,\sigma^2)$ and σ^2 is unknown. The best fitted model is a linear model and which is

$$y = 641.814 - 1.8143X$$

with R^2 equal to 0.075, where R^2 is the residual sum of square. The next suitable model is an exponential as $y = 639.12e^{-0.003x}$ but its residual sum of squares (= 0.078) which is more than R^2 of linear model.

Similarly, a best model can be fitted for total deaths. Let death of children is a dependent variable; say y, and month say X as independent variable. In this case also, the linear model provides the best fit for the total deaths data. Let the linear model is

$$y_i = \beta_0 + \beta_1 x_i + \epsilon_i \; ; i=1, 2,..., 36$$

where ϵ_i***'s*** are identically independently distributed $N(0,\sigma^2)$ and σ^2 is unknown. Applying the method of least squares, the parameters β_0 and $\beta_1$are estimated and therefore the best fit becomes

$$y = 64.5333 - 0.0784\,x$$

The value of residual sum of squares *i.e.* R^2 is 0.005. Here, both the said models are fitted with the help of 36 months data which was available from the health department. It gives an idea of change in live births and deaths of children as months vary.

In the section 3.3, the null hypothesis H_{03} and H_{04} are assumed and which are tested on the basis of the data given in Table 3.5. This is a two - way classified data with three observations per month. After completing all the necessary computational work, the final ANOVA table has been prepared and presented as Table 3.7. As F calculated for interaction between seasons and number of deaths in different age-groups is more than F tabulated at 5% level of significance, therefore it can be concluded that, there is a significant interaction effect. The F calculated are greater than F tabulated at 5% level of significance for both, effect of seasons as well as for different age-groups, hence the null hypothesis H_{01} and H_{04} are rejected. That is, there is a significant effect of seasons on the number of deaths and also there is a significant difference in different age-groups due to malnutrition deaths.

Table 3.7: ANOVA table for Seasons (S) and Age- groups (Ag)

s.v.	*d.f.*	*SS*	*MSS*	F_{cal}	F_{tab}
SSS	11	1005	91.32513	4.419	1.89
SSAg	3	6264	2088.081	101	2.7
SSIr	33	1193	36.14668	1.749	1.56
SSH	96	1984	20.66667		
Total	143	10446			

Now, it is needed to find the difference between the seasons which affect the deaths and between the grades which differ since both the hypothesis are rejected.

The pair-wise differences of all the months have been calculated after arranging the means in descending order and presented in Table 3.8. The least significant difference *i.e.,* critical difference is 5.34 at 5% level of significance for error degree of freedom. Comparing the calculated difference from Table 3.8 with CD, we can see that July

Table 3.8: Mean Difference table for Seasons

Treatment	*Mean*	*Aug.*	*Sep.*	*Jan.*	*Jul.*
Aug.	06	0	–	–	–
Sep.	56.75	9.25	0	–	–
Jan.	52.25	13.75	4.5	0	–
Jul.	49.75	16.25	7	2.5	0
Jun.	45	21	11.75	7.25	4.75
Nov.	45	21	11.75	7.25	4.75
Dec.	44.5	21.5	12.25	7.75	5.25
Feb.	43.5	22.5	13.25	8.75	6.25
March .	43.5	22.5	13.25	8.75	6.25
Oct.	43.5	22.5	13.25	8.75	6.25
May.	40.5	25.5	16.25	11.75	9.25
Apr.	34	32	22.75	18.25	15.75

	Jun.	*Nov.*	*Dec.*	*Feb.*	*Mar.*	*Oct.*	*May*	*Apr.*
Nov.	0	0						
Dec.	0.5	0.5	0					
Feb.	1.5	1.5	1	0				
March.	1.5	1.5	1	0	0			
Oct.	1.5	1.5	1	0	0	0		
May.	4.5	4.5	4	3	3	3	0	
Apr.	11	11	10.5	9.5	9.5	9.5	6.5	0

CD. at 5 % level of significance for seasons 5.336153

does not differ significantly with January, June, November. Similarly, June, November, December, February, March, October and May do not differ significantly pair-wise with each other. Except these, all the other remaining pair of months differs significantly from each other.

The difference of means between different age groups have been calculated and presented in Table 3.9. Also, the value of critical difference has been calculated at 5% level of significance for error degree of freedom which is 3.08. From the Table 3.9, it can be easily observed, comparing these differences with the CD that all the values are more than CD. Therefore, all the age-groups differ significantly from each other.

Table 3.9: Mean difference table for ages Treatment

Treatment	*Mean*	*Age 01*	*Age 00*	*Age 13*	*Age 36*
age 01	66.833	0			
age 00	61.75	5.083	0		
age 13	43.167	23.67	18.5833	0	
age 36	16.333	50.5	45.4167	26.83	0

CD. at 5% level of significance for age = 3.08083

There are births and deaths in every month which affects the total population of the children between 0-6 age group. With the help of the available data, a mathematical relation can be obtained between these three variables. Here, total population of children (Y) is a dependent variable and births (X_1) and deaths (X_2) are independent variables. Suppose, the model between them is,

$$y_i = \beta_0+\beta_1 x_1+\beta_2 x_2+\epsilon_i;\ i=1, 2,..., 36$$

where ϵ_i***'s*** are identically independently distributed $N(0,\sigma^2)$ and σ^2 is unknown. Applying the method of least squares, the parameters β_0, β_1 and β_2 can be estimated. The best fitted model is,

$$y = 38684.525 + 4.266\ x_1 - 7.903\ x_2$$

The value of residual sum of squares is 0.061. This model can be used for predicting the total population of

House in Melghat (*Source* – Nayak, 2012)

House in Melghat (*Source* – Nayak, 2012)

the children between 0-6 years age group with the help of number of live births and deaths in every month.

3.5. Findings

It is clear that the government is offering various welfare schemes to the tribals in Melghat region and also,

Farming in Melghat (*Source* – Nayak, 2012)

House in Melghat (*Source* – Nayak, 2012)

providing sufficient medical aids. Even though, children are either malnourished or dying. The percentages of malnourished children of different categories are high. The effect of different seasons on the number of deaths due to malnutrition is significant.

4

General Profile of The Respondents

4.1. INTRODUCTION

The previous chapter has revealed the fact that the government is providing a number of facilities and running several schemes in the Melghat region, even then the children are dying due to malnourishment. Also, a lot of children are presently suffering due to malnutrition. To study the different aspects of the possible reasons the data has been collected and analysed. Our questionnaire consists of three parts and first is general information. The same has been analysed and presented in this chapter.

The purpose of collecting data of the general profile of the respondents is very simple and clear (see Pande, 1989b). This helps the author to understand the overall background of the respondent. It also explains as to what are the situational factors that constitute the profile of the average representative respondents. Certain factors considered in the general profile also explain as to the social background and certain personality related traits of the respondents.

The questions regarding age, sex, family size, etc, are useful to understand in what age group the general respondents fall. It also helps the author to know, what are the attitude related factors governing the respondents, such as age and family size, which are the factors that throw light on social set-up, value system and respondents view towards the factors. Age at the time of marriage of male and female also helps to establish relationship between family size and average age of the general period of fertility and the possible number of children in a particular family.

Educational qualification is one factor that helps to examine the association between level of literacy, family size, value system, number of dependents and approach towards childcare. Often education is the most crucial factor that changes social conventions, approach towards personal, physical and social problems. Usually educated societies have a more elevated social value structure. People become more health conscious and inclined towards materialistic pleasures. Hence, study of educational factors has a great relevance in this research.

Type of dwellings indicates the socio-economic status, income level, as well as a preventive mechanism available to protect the health and property of respondents. This also helps to know whether the respondents are prone to a higher level of natural and physical hazards.

This chapter deals with the general information about the households of Melghat region. It gives the general information about the families of the respondents. Here, we have tried to find out the average age of the head of the house and also whether the majority of the heads of the houses are male or female. Then an attempt is made to find the average age of the husband and wife at marriage. Also, an attempt is made to find some of the inferences about the difference of age of the husband and wife. The educational status of both husband and wife has also been assessed. The study is also made about the types of houses they live in and the size of their family. The information is also collected regarding religion, caste and language (cf. Banerjee, 1964).

4.2. THE BASIS OF QUESTIONS

The term household is a basic unit in statistical demography. The term 'house-hold' concerns with all members in a house, who share a common kitchen (chullah) and live under a single roof. We demographers consider household as the unit of enquiry because it gives more elaborate description of natural group in which people live. Total 300 households are randomly chosen and their information is collected in the form of data, here for this study.

Sex and Age Compositions

Sex and age are both biological factors. Moreover, they are independent variables which are necessary for almost all classifications related to population characteristics. Sex and age structure of a population defines the limits of a society's reproductive potential. This structure is also the basic demographic determinant of a country's manpower reserve.

The sex and age structure of a population at any given time is the outcome of its trends in fertility, mortality and territorial movement in the past. It, in turn, influences contemporary levels of birth and death rates and the rate of future population growth.

Sex Composition

Communities differ in sex composition *i.e.,* composition of number of males and females. It is of fundamental importance, both socially and demographically. Sex composition affects directly birth rate, death rate and marriage. It appears as a differential in marital status and occupational distribution.

In any given area the distribution of sexes tends to be unequal owing to the operation of any of the following factors.

(i) A differentiation in sex at birth is universal. More males are born every where than females.

(ii) The death rate of males is usually higher than those of females at all ages.

(iii) Migration is sex selective. In long distance movements, males tend to out number females but in short distance movements females usually predominate.

Sex Ratio (SR) can be calculated as number of females per thousand males

$$SR = \frac{\text{Number of females}}{\text{Number of males}} \times 1000$$

The survey of 2001 reveals that the total number of males and females in Melghat region are 124 and 119 thousand, respectively. Therefore, the sex ratio in this region is 960 approximately.

Age Composition

The age structure of population is the basic concept of population composition. Almost every aspect of human behavior, physical capabilities, mental maturity and attitude objectives, are the characteristics which vary with the age attained. The extensive change in age composition results in adaptive changes in many areas of its behavior. Its influence is more conspicuous in the composition of labour force. Thus, the age composition of the population constitutes the framework, on which the institutional structure of the entire society rests.

The age composition of a population is a product of the birth, death and migration factors. It is biologically related to "fertility and mortality". Birth rates and death rates can meaningfully be compared and interpreted only when age and sex composition of population is taken into consideration. In non-literate areas, such as present area of study, individuals often do not remember their correct date year of birth. Thus, data on age is less reliable than sex data. It has been seen that the respondents have a tendency to concentrate on the numbers ending with zero and five.

Marital Status

One of the basic functions of a society is to reproduce itself. As human societies differentiate between mating and reproduction through marriage, the institution of marriage has been found to be universal. This has been further reinforced by social and cultural factors of each society which, in turn, determines the forms as well as the rules of marriage. Some societies enjoin to their people early marriages of their men and women whereas some others prescribe late marriages. Thus, the social structure of different societies has greatly influenced the marriage pattern around the world. Among the Hindus, who form more than 80 percent of the country's population, the primary role of the woman has remained that of a mother and every man is ordained to marry in order that his family is perpetuated through son. Even in other religious communities like Muslims, Sikhs and Christians, the practice of universal marriage is quite prevalent in the country.

Marital status in a population varies significantly with age and sex. In countries where the population has comparatively larger proportion of young population, the proportion of never married persons can be higher provided the age of marriage is not very low. If the population has a comparatively older structure the proportion of never married persons will be low.

Further, the social structure of different societies has greatly influenced the marriage pattern around the world. For example, we find polygamy among the Muslims, which probably creates greater differentials between the average age of the bride groom and the bride at the time of marriage. In communities where child marriages are still quite prevalent, the proportion of never married is expected to be low.

Marital status as an element of composition of study is of considerable importance. It immediately provides an idea about reproduction. Differences in marital status have direct bearing on both fertility and mortality. The age at which people get married and the proportion of the population that actually gets married are an important determinant of the fertility. It has been generally observed that Fertility is higher in places where marriages are concluded early and where the proportion of marriages is high. Mortality also varies with marital status, both married males and married females have lower death rate than unmarried persons of the same age. In fact, these differentials arise from the reason that marriage is selective or the greater longevity of marriage may result from the better personal care and greater regularity.

When viewed comparatively such data are useful indicators of social, economic and cultural differences among different populations. The information about the marital status is generally included by demographers in their study as it has many advantages. Considering these facts, in our study also, it has been incorporated.

Age of Marriage

One important aspect of the study of the marital status of any given population is to know the average age of the bride-groom and the bride at the time of marriage. This aspect becomes important in human societies because reproduction basically takes place in wedlock. Moreover, in societies where early marriages are prevalent, one finds that, on an average, a woman bears a greater number of children during her child bearing span as compared to those where late marriages are prevalent (Chandan, 1990) and Gopalan, 1987).

In India, girls marry early and universally. This pattern is due to "feasibility" and "desirability" of marriage. "Feasibility" is determined primarily by expectations of financial and residential independence of the couple, including down requirements and by the availability of resources. It is obvious that, marriage is feasible under the joint family system and Indian low conditions of living. "Desirability" is determined by the availability of social and institutional alternatives to marriage, child bearing and by the extent to which these alternatives are considered rewarding. Under this category, we should consider, "the penalties of marrying late or never, in particular the penalties of childlessness, social rotation and stigma, and the loss of opportunities for economic support and social mobility (especially important for women)". This situation prevailing in India on these matters is such that marriage has become universal (Jain, 1975).

In the Melghat region, the marriage is universal and the age at marriage is not generally decided on the basis of feasibility.

Educational Status

A person is regarded as literate if he or she is able to read and write a simple message with understanding it in any language. The literacy rate of the population (see Hansraj, 1996), can be defined as.

$$\text{Literacy Rate} = \frac{\text{Number of literate persons of specified sex and area}}{\text{Population of persons of that sex and area}} \times 100$$

The information regarding the number of literate persons of both sex is available as per census report 2001 of Melghat region. The numbers of literate male and female are 75631 and 48485, respectively in the whole region, whereas the total populations of male and female are 124 and 119 thousands respectively. Therefore, the literacy rate of male and female can easily be calculated by using the above formulae. The literacy rate of male and female is 609.93 and 407.44, respectively. Here, it is evident that female literacy rate is quite below the male literacy rate.

As a demographic characteristic, educational status is used as an index of well being of socio-economic position or in general of the degree of familiarity" with culture and the receptivity to new ideas and information on the part of individuals. The importance of education in the modern world is so evident that it needs no exposition (Madan, 1951) and Raza *et al.,* 1990). In other words, educational status has direct relevance for a wide array of concerns, ranging from measurement of fertility, mortality and other demographic events to the inventories of the human resources of societies and the possibility of systematic social changes. It is for such reason that educational data are collected. The educational status of the people is also one of the most important cultural variables which influence the reproductive behaviour of the people. The various studies have shown positive relationship between educational attainments of households and their outlook towards the size of family, age at marriage, attitude towards use of contraception, etc. (see Mohanty, 1970).

Hussain (1972) has claimed that there exists following types of relationships

(i) A positive relationship between the educational attainment of the household members including its head and the mean age at marriage of males and females.

(ii) A strong negative relationship between fertility and educational status of the household.

(iii) Direct relationship of preference of 2 or 3 children with the educational level of head and household members, and

(iv) An increase in the proportion of opinion in favour of liberalisation of abortion laws with a rise in educational status.

Although the people in Melghat have little benefit of higher education yet status of their education is being improved slowly.

Types of Houses

The houses here are generally damp, insufficiently ventilated, over crowded and devoid of the most rudimentary sanitary facilities, which attracts malaria or respiratory diseases, etc. During the collection of data period, general discussions with the people revealed the fact that the diseases common among them are malaria, venereal diseases, gastric disorders, skin diseases and tuberculosis. The incidence of malarial fever is mainly responsible for most of the mortality and also a large proportion of population suffers from malarial cachexia. The causes of the diseases may be attributed to imbalanced diet, malnutrition, polluted drinking water and other insanitary unhygienic habits.

Family Size

In the advanced western societies where Planned Parenthood is a way of life, data on expected family size have great significance. Even their, family size preferences change with time under the impact of social as well as economic changes during the course of married life. Such changes particularly affect preferences formed early in marriage, as occupational carrier is unfolded and the wife gains experience of child bearing. Bumpass and Westoff (1975) have found from their study that the number of children desired after the birth of the second child predicts the average completed family size variable. The desire formed at this stage constitutes meaningful goals, in terms of which the respondents regulate their subsequent behaviour. However, the position in India in general and in Melghat in particular is very- different. There is a wide gap between the preferred family size and the actual family size. The actual family size becomes much larger than the desired or ideal size due to desire for sons. Most of the surveys show the preferred size, to be of three children in urban areas and of four in the rural areas (see Basu, 1993a) and Sinha, 1990). Yet large families are most common.

4.3. MODELING OF FAMILY SIZE

The study of total family size can be done more appropriately if a statistical probability distribution can be established. Such model will help in drawing inference prediction about family sizes in this region. Let 'X' denotes a random variable which defines the number of family members in a family, n is a positive integer which is the total family size and $p = P(X = x)$ is the probability of x members in a family. Here, the probability mass function (p.m.f.) and cumulative distribution function (c.d.f.) of X can be defined as.

$$P_B(X = x) = \binom{n}{x}.p^x q_n \; ; \; X=0,1,2,\ldots,n \quad ** (4.1)$$

and

$$F_B(x) = \sum_{k=0}^{x} \binom{n}{k}.p^k q^{n-k} \quad *** (4.2)$$

where $q = 1 - p$, n and p are the parameters (for detail see Johnson and Kotz, 1970). The testing of fitting of this model on our collected data will be done in the next section.

4.4. ANALYSIS OF DATA

The general profile of the questionnaire enclosed in Appendix "A" has been completed by asking the answers to the respondents and the same has been classified and presented in the tabular form at the end of this chapter. The Table 4.1, gives the frequency distribution of the family heads age. From this table it is clear that the maximum numbers of family heads are between the age

Table 4.1: Frequency Distribution of Family Head's age

Age	*Frequency*	*Percent*
10-20	1	0.3
20-30	62	20.7
30-40	90	30.0
40-50	68	22.7
50-60	41	13.7
60-70	29	9.7
70-80	8	2.7
80-90	1	0.3
	Mean = 44.09	Max. = 85
	S. D. = 13.95	Min. = 17
	Van = 194.58	

group of 30-40 that is 90, which is 30 percent of the collected data. The number of persons *i.e.,* 68 and 62 are the family heads of the age interval 40-50 and 20-30, respectively. It shows that the house heads are mostly young persons or moderately middle-aged. It has also been observed that the head of the family may in 'most of the cases' be males whatever age group they may belong. In an example of the same we have found that an old female respondent has named her grandson of 17 years of age as the family head. The maximum age of the family head has been observed that of 85 years. The average age of the family heads is 44.09 years with a standard deviation of 13.95 years. Table 4.2, provides the sex of family heads. It is clear from the table that, in 95 percent cases the family heads are males and remaining 5 percent are females. That is, out of 300 surveyed families, 285 males are family heads and 15 are females. It is evident from the above discussions that patriarchy is prevalent in this region.

Table 4.2: Frequency Distribution of Family Head's

Sex	*Frequency*	*Percent*
F	15	5
M	285	95

The frequency distribution of the respondents age is presented in Table 4.3, the sex of the respondents in Table 4.4 and frequency distribution of their marital status in Table 4.5. Since, our problem is related to the death of children due to malnutrition, we have tried to ask the responses from young and married male or female. From the Table 4.3, we can see that 130 *i.e.,* 43.3 percent respondents belong to the age-group of 20-30 years. Similarly, 78 *i.e.,* 26 percent and 38 *i.e.,* 12.7 percent

Table 4.3: Frequency Distribution of Respondent's

Age	*Frequency*	*Percent*
10-20	38	12.7
20-30	130	43.3
30-40	78	26.0
40-50	23	7.7
50-60	19	6.3
60-70	8	2.7
70-80	4	1.3
	Mean = 32.60	Max. = 80
	S.D. = 13.15	Min. = 14
	Var. = 172.983	

respondents belong to 30-40 and below 20 years age-group, respectively. Here, 82 percent of the respondents are below 40 years. In this region most of the people are farmers or farm labours. So, many times it was difficult to find young married men and women at home because they were out to work in the fields. Thus, we were in many cases forced to select the respondents of the older age-group who were available at home, but the percentage of such respondents is very less. In such cases, we have tried to get the required information of that family through these people. The average age, of the respondents is 32.6 years with a standard deviation of 13.15 years. The minimum and maximum ages of the respondents are 14 and 80, respectively.

Table 4.4 shows that 69.3 percent *i.e.,* a total of 208 out of 300 respondents are male and 30.7 percent *i.e.,* 92 are female. The male respondents were easily accessible and came forward to give the answer about their household easily whereas the females of the house were generally shy, may be due to illiteracy and did not want to come forward. The percentage of married respondents is 84 percent (see Table 4.5). As discussed earlier 14 percent unmarried respondents have been questioned about the family information just because of non-availability of proper person of that household. It is meaningless to mention here, a proper care has been taken while considering as a respondent an unmarried person, that he was an adult.

Table 4.4: Frequency distribution of respondent's sex

	Frequency	***Percent***
F	92	30.7
M	208	69.3

Table 4.5: Frequency distribution of respondent's marital status

	Frequency	***Percent***
Married	252	84.0
Unmarried	42	14.0
Widow	6	2.0

The age at marriage of a couple is important and it decides their future family size. In fact, the early marriage gives larger span of child bearing age and which increases the probability of having more number of children. The collected data has been summarised in Table 4.6. From this table, we can see that the maximum male *i.e.,* 135 have married at the age between 18 to 21. It means, 45 percent of husbands have been married in the age-group of 18 to 21 whereas 21.33 *i.e.,* 10 percent have been married between 21 to 24 and after 24, respectively. The marriages even before achieving 18 years of age have also been observed. Surprisingly, 7 cases have been seen where the husbands were married as young as 12 to 15 years age-group. It is worthy to mention that 56 percent marriages have taken place even when husbands were not eligible

Table 4.6: Frequency distribution of husband's and wife's marriageable age <GBG(MA)

Wife's M.A.	*NA*	*12-15*	*15-18*	*18-21*	*21-24*	*>24*	*Total*	*Percent*
NA	38	0	0	0	0	0	38	12.6667
12-15	0	6	7	10	0	0	23	7.66667
15-18	0	1	15	74 —	13	6	109	36.3333
18-21	0	0	4	46	49	12	111	37
21-24	0	0	0	2	2	11	15	5
>24	0	0	0	3	0	1	4	1.33333
Total	38	7	26	135	64	30	300	
Percent	12.66	2.33	8.66	45.00	21.33	10.00		

HM Age: Mean = 17.87; S.D. = 7.2680; Var. = 52.824; WM Age: Mean = 15.6650; r=0.5367; S.D. = 6.4579; Var = 41.704

as per government Rules *i.e.,* without completing 21 years of age. The average age of a male at marriage is 17.87 years with standard deviation of 7.27 years.

The women of this region are generally married any how before 21 years of age. From the table, we can observe that 109 *i.e.,* 36.33 percent and 111 *i.e.* 37 percent females have been married between 15 to 18 and 18 to 21 years, respectively. Twenty-three women have been married between 12 to 15 years of the age and thus 44 percent wives were married even before 18 years which is the minimum age of marriage for a woman as per government rules. Thirty-eight respondents could not answer about their (both husband and wife) age at marriage due to marriage at a very young age as well as illiteracy. A woman at an average age of 15.67 years gets married and its standard deviation is 6.46 years.

From the above discussions it is clear that both male and female get married at an early age. To study the relation, correlation coefficient has been obtained which is 0.54. In very few cases it has also been observed that the wives are a little older than their husbands, but in most of the cases generally wives are younger.

The educational qualification of husband as well as wife plays very crucial role in the family's welfare. As discussed earlier, it is a general observation that a qualified mother deals more properly the family matters and brings up children well. If both husband and wife are educated then it becomes more advantageous. To see this, the data of educational qualification of husband (HEQ) and wife (WEQ) has been collected, summarised and presented in Table 4.7.

Table 4.7: Frequency distribution of Husband's (H) and wife's (W) educational qualification (EQ)

	HEQ									
WEQ	***NA***	***IL***	***Literate***	***4th***	***7th***	***10th fail***	***10th pass***	***Other***	***Total***	***Percent***
NA	1	11	1	4	11	4	3	6	31	10.3333
IL	0	59	30	33	12	3	3	4	144	48
Functional Literate	o	2	22	15	6	4	3	2	54	18
4th	<	2	4	14	11	6	0	4	41	13.6667
7th	0	2	0	0	2	5	3	3	15	5
10th Fail	0	0	0	0	0	0	2	2	4	1.33333
10th Pass	0	1	0	0	2	o	2	3	8	2.66667
Others	1	0	0	0	1	0	0	1	3	1
Total	2	67	57	66	45	22	16	25	300	
Percent	0.66	22.33	19	22	15	7.33	5.33	8.33		

From the table, we can observe that a large number of husbands are illiterate *i.e.,* 67 which is 22.33 percent of the total population. Also, the numbers of 4th pass husbands are nearly equal to illiterate *i.e.,* 66. It can be seen that the number of persons who have never taken any formal education but know reading and writing *i.e.,* functional literate are significantly high which is 57 (19 percent of total population). Therefore, it is evident that most of the husbands are illiterate or below 7th class pass and thus the total percentage of seventh pass or less qualified is 78.33 percent. Hence, the literacy in the married male is not very high.

The Table 4.7 also provides the information of educational status of wives. The illiterate wives are maximum and their percentage is 48 percent. The percentages of functional literate and 4th class pass wives are 18 and 13.66, respectively. Thirty-one respondents have not answered about the wives qualification and this may be due to their illiteracy. Therefore, 90 percent wives are either 4th class pass or less qualified. Here, it is clear that literacy in married females is much less than males who themselves are not much qualified.

Let us now consider the hypothesis that there is no association between husband's education and wives education. To test this hypothesis, chi-square test has been applied. The calculated value of chi-square is 5.6893, which is very high to tabulated value of chi-square *i.e.,* 19.675 at 5 percent level of significance. Thus, the assumed hypothesis is rejected and there is a significant association between husbands and wives educational status. That is less qualified husbands are married to even less qualified wives. To measure the association between education of husband and wife, Tschuprow's coefficient of association has been calculated which is 0.0562201. This also shows that there is a positive association.

The caste wise details of frequency distribution are presented in Table 4.8. This table shows that 213Z *i.e.,* 71

Table 4.8: Caste-wise frequency distribution

Caste	***Frequency***	***Percent***
Bhavsar	1	0.3
Balai	7	2.3
Basor	5	1.7
Budha	12	4.0
Gaulan	21	7.0
Gawali	22	7.3
Gond	10	3.3
Kalal	2	0.7
Katwal	1	0.3
Koli	1	0.3
Korku	213	71.0
Mahar	2	0.7
Maratha	1	0.3
Nhavi	1	0.3
Patil	1	0.3
Total	**300**	

percent population is of Korkus. The Korkus are scheduled tribes and the whole region is mainly populated by Korkus. The population of other castes such as Bhavsar, Balai, Basor, Buddha, Gond, Kalal, Koli, Mahar, Maratha and Nhavi are very nominal, but Gawalis and Gaulans also exist in a little more numbers in some villages. Thus, Korkus are the main inhibitors of this area.

The Table 4.9 shows the frequency distribution of the types of houses in which the people of Melghat region live. This is another very important factor which affects the life of the people and causes the diseases which may be fatal. From this table, we observe that 47.7 percent people live in the temporary huts made from grass, mud. etc. Thirty-five percent of the population lives in Parched hutment. Permanent bamboo constructed huts are

Table 4.9: Frequency Distribution of type of house

Type	*Frequency*	*Percent*
Temp. hut.	143	47.7
Perm.B.C.	8	2.7
Par. Hut.	105	35.0
Te.M&SC.	10	3.3
Perm.Dw.	22	7.3
Others	12	4.0
Total	**300**	

Note: For details of abbreviations see question number 7 of Part -1 of questionnaire in Appendix 'A'.

minimum and only 8 such kind of huts have been seen out of total 300 cases. The 7.3 percent houses are permanent dwellings made of bricks and cement. And this percentage is meager. Therefore, majority of families are living in temporary and damp houses which may be causing health problems for them.

The data regarding the total number of members in a family has been collected and its frequency distribution is given in the Table 4.10. The study of this family size becomes important because this gives an idea regarding availability of sufficient meals to each family member. If

Table 4.10: Frequency Distribution of total Family members

Class-Int	*Frequency*	*Percent*
2-4	89	29.7
4-6	140	46.7
6-8	56	18.7
8-10	7	2.3
10-12	5	1.7
12-14	2	0.7
>14	1	0.3

Mean = 5.56 Min. = 2 Var. = 7.485 Max. = 40 S.D. = 2.74

the number of family members will be more then it will be difficult for house-heads to provide complete and nutritious foods to every member. Our collected data reveals that 46.7 percent families' *i.e.,* maximum families are of 4 to 6 members (see Table 4.10). The number of families of size between 2 to 4 and 6 to 8 are 29.7 and 18.7 percent, respectively. Most of the families are not joint families. We have also encountered a household having 40 members (joint family) in it. We have also seen several families having number of members ranging from 8 to 14 (see Table 4.10 for their percentages). In fact, during our personal visit to villages for Survey work we have experienced that the families which could not be selected in our random sample were having much more number of family members contradicting the data of Table 4.10. This was so because we have mostly selected randomly the young couples who were still in their child-bearing age, (see Table 4.3).

To test the fitting of distribution (4.1) on the data of Table 4.10, the chi-square method of goodness of fit has been applied, the estimated value of parameter p is 0.4186 and the p-value comes out to be 0.2078 which is more than 0.05. This shows, the hypothesis that the family size follows a Binomial distribution, is accepted. Hence, the Binomial distribution is an appropriate model for family size.

Findings

From the above analysis we can conclude that Korkus are the main constituent of the population of this region. The marriages take place at a very young age, even without completing the minimum age limit. This gives larger span of child bearing age and couples reproduce more children. Moreover, they are mostly illiterate in general. Some

House in Melghat (*Source* – Nayak, 2012)

Status of Girl child in Melghat (*Source* – Nayak, 2012)

significant population has functional knowledge of writing and reading without taking any formal education. Their houses are not in good position, damp and unhygienic. These conditions make the houses, to attract diseases. Above all their family sizes are also big and follow the Binomial probability law. Due to all these, they are unable to have proper living conditions and food.

5

Conditions Governing Economic Status

5.1. INTRODUCTION

The prosperity of the society can be assessed by their economic status. This economic status depends on the geographical situation where a particular society" lives. Therefore, economic prosperity is the result of resource availability, income generation capacity and level of employment, etc.. No society advances without favourable economic conditions (Rostow, 1960). A society where conditions are not favourable, economic prosperity is usually missing (Anstey, 1942) and Simon, 1983). In the Melghat region, the population is mainly tribal and primitive. Their level of resource utilization is very poor and overall income generation levels are at their low ebbs. Under such circumstances societies remain undeveloped and personal income generation is very poor. Low personal income leads to low per capita income which affects consumption pattern, educational level and social personal health (Gupta, 1976); Srivastava and Chaturvedi, 1989).

Poor economic conditions work against social and economic interest of the individuals. They cannot avail the advantage of technology and convert the techno-educational advancement into social benefits. These result in widening the gap between the advanced and backward societies (Paul, 1952).

For the purpose of the present work regarding economic parameters which affects the nutritional status of the children of Melghat region, the following 10 factors have been considered as basic indicators of the economic conditions of the tribals (see for details. Bern- (1965), Boeke (1976), Clarke (1951), Gerschenkron (1962) and Lerner (1958), etc.). These factors are –

(1) Occupation,

(2) Annual Income,

(3) Farming and ownership of land,

(4) Animal Husbandry,

(5) Income generation from animal rearing,

(6) Monthly expenses on various things like food, clothes, medicines, shelter, etc.,

(7) Gap between Income and Expenses,

(8) Subsidiary and financial assistance from government,

(9) Nature of subsidiary and financial assistance,

(10) Amount of subsidiary and financial assistance.

—

Considering these factors the inference regarding income, expenses and economic status of the population in Melghat region has been drawn. With the help of this inference an attempt is made to understand the basis of malnutrition as well as infant mortality.

5.2. ECONOMIC FACTORS

Melghat region is rich in natural wealth and minerals. But the people are poor and backward. They have little control over the resources of their own area, which has brought a sense of alienation and hopelessness among them. The main economic problems that this area is tackling are the problems of poverty, income-inequalities, unemployment and under-employment (see Mandal, 1961). Their economic status can be studied with the help of their occupation, earnings, farming, animal husbandry, expenditure and government support, etc..

5.2.1. Occupational Composition

The pattern of occupation signifies the general structure of economy, level of living, involvement of persons in different activities. In a predominantly agricultural country, agriculture stands as the mainstay of economy. Probably, the tribal economy may not be an exception to this rule. Other than agriculture, the occupation of people of this region are hunting, dairy, forest labour, fishing, farming, farm labour, sheep raring, collecting wax and honey. Vaidh, Mantrik, others (Shanna, 1987).

5.2.2. Earning

The yearly income is the most important factor to study

the economical status of the people of this region. The sources of their income are the occupations discussed in the previous sub-section. In fact, they earn through selling their crops in the form of grains, selling milk, selling the products collected from the forest, service, labour charges and animal husbandry, etc.. The main sources of income of the families are earnings by husband, wife, children and other close relatives living in the same household.

Italian born, Swiss Professor of Economics, Vilfredo Pareto (1897) has suggested an income model, whose probability distribution function is,

$$F_p(x)=1- \left(\frac{k}{x}\right)^{\alpha} \quad , \alpha > 0, {}^{\alpha} > 0, x \geq k \qquad *** \qquad (5.1)$$

It was felt by Pareto that this law was universal and inevitable-regardless of taxation and social and political condition.

Land Ownership

Most of the tribal populations have been found to be dependent on agriculture, but the agricultural conditions among them are miserably poor. In this region, the farmers are subject to the vagaries of monsoon and the irrigation facilities are almost absent. Heavy intensity of soil erosion and inhospitable terrain, etc. keep it below the subsistence level. Since it seems, the main occupation and the major source of income of a large majority of population is agriculture and in order to improve the economic conditions, the major emphasis is required to be given on the development of agriculture.

The returns from agriculture are very poor in this area because of:

(1) Poor quality of land which is usually undulating, hilly and marginal,

(2) Very primitive technology, and

(3) Almost complete dependence on rains and complete lack of irrigation facilities.

The tribals also have many different ways of getting a farming land. The land on which they are farming may be their own, or it may be the whole families land on which everybody of the family works, or they may have received it from their ancestors, or it may even be a land belonging to the whole clan, or they might have a land received from the government. Taking into account the special tribal customs and traditions regarding ownership of land, various laws and statutes enacted by the state government, the question about the ownership of the land becomes important.

Forestry

Forest is a major source of income to the tribals of this region. Indeed in main-areas, the whole economy is based on forests. The people collect the medicinal plants, wax, honey, tendu leaves, mohua, etc. and sell these to generate livelihood. They use the dried parts of the forest trees as fuel for cooking.

Animal Husbandry

Tribal agriculture particularly in the Melghat region continues to be based primarily on animal power. The people give considerable importance to the animals and the status of the families sometimes is determined in many communities by the number of cattle owned. The animals are used mainly for the purpose of agricultural work and for small distance transportation of agricultural products. Besides, being used in agricultural operations, animals have been useful for raising the level of diet and providing adequate protein and also a source of subsidiary income. Improvement in the cattle wealth would also need suitable nutrition support for them, it is also difficult to arrange for supply on an extensive scale of cattle feed in inaccessible regions in Melghat area.

5.2.3. Expenditure

The people of Melghat region generally spend less money per month. Their expenditure is on food, clothing, maintenance of houses, medicines, farming, animals, festival, etc.. Their expenditures on purchasing are less compared to others since they have an exchange system of goods. This exchange (give and take) system makes the economic management of this region very simple and also instead of monetary transaction the people here prefer the exchange of commodities. So, there are only necessary and limited things in their households. Here, even the labour charges are given and taken in the form of grains. But, it seems now-a-days because of their connections and knowledge about the outer world *i.e.*, nearby cities, they have started relying less on this system. Still this system is in practice. It is important here to study the different heads of expenditure in order to assess their status of living as well as their opinion about the heads for which their income is insufficient.

5.2.4. Government's Financial Aids

The central government as well as state government are running a number of schemes for the benefit of people of this region which has already been discussed in section 3.1. The state Government of Maharashtra also provides financial support. The main type of aid is known as Khauti. Under this scheme, the Government provides these people during the rainy season, one sack of food grain at subsidized rate. The government also gives them loans at very low interest rates for different purposes such as for buying agricultural land, house, bullocks, bullock-carts, cows, buffaloes, etc..

5.3. ANALYSIS OF ECONOMIC DATA

The factors affecting the economical status of the people, which have been discussed in the section 5.2 of this chapter, have been used to frame the various questions which have been asked from the respondents. These questions can be seen in the questionnaire which is enclosed in Appendix "A". The responses have been summarised and presented in the various tables from Table 5.1 to Table 5.8.

The data collected regarding profession or occupation is presented in the Table 5.1. From the table, we can see that the majority of people are based on farming business and their percentage is 53.66 percent. Nearly 30 percent are farm labours, which occupation is next to farming. This can also be confirmed from the responses of question 3 of the economic part of questionnaire (see appendix "A") that 57 percent of the respondents have answered 'yes' for their earning source from the farms, (see Sr. No. 1 of Table

Table 5.1: Frequency distribution of different occupations

Sl. no.	*Profession*	*Frequency*	*Percent*
1	Hunting	0	0
2	Dairy	11	3.6666667
3	Forest labour	33	11
4	Fishing	2	0.6666667
5	Farming	161	53.666667
6	Farm labour	91	30.333333
7	Sheep raring	9	3
8	Collecting wax & Honey	5	1.6666667
9	Vaidh	0	0
10	Mantrik	1	0.3333333
11	Others	26	8.6666667

5.8). It can be seen that 11 percent are forest labours and therefore the total percentage of labours becomes 41 percent. In this region, the percentage of other professions such as dairy business, sheep raring, collecting wax and honey fishing, etc. are very nominal. It is generally felt that the tribal people are engaged in hunting and as Vaidh. But in our samples we could not find any respondent or his family members practicing these two occupations. It is very hard to conclude that the tribals are not in these two professions, but it may be possible that there may be few people doing these. It may be due to very hard government prohibition rule that hunting is restricted. The reason for non-existence or limited number of Vaidh may be due to availability of health centres and other medical facilities. But one Mantrik has been found in our collected data and this shows that the practice of "Tantra-Mantra" is still in existence in this region, which may also be limited. It has also been noted that some people of this region have some supporting occupation other than their main profession.

The income from various sources like; earning of husband, wife, children and others, in which the parents or siblings earning have been considered to study the economical status of a household. This is because a high-earning family may be having better living conditions. The related earning data are presented in the Tables 5.2.1 to 5.2.6. The first table that is 5.2.1 gives the frequency distribution of husband's earning per year. From the table we can see that the earning is distributed from 0 to 96,000 in a year. In one case, we met a person of service class whose earning was 96,000 whereas in a number of cases the earning was nil due to unemployment. Nearly 26 percent husbands are annually earning between Rs. 2000 to 3000, 21 percent between Rs.3000 to 4000 and 12 percent between Rs. 4000 to 5000. The average earning is Rs. 5733 per annum with a standard deviation of Rs.

Table 5.2.1: Frequency distribution of Husband's Yearly Income (HY1)

Interval (Rs.)	*Frequency*	*Percent*
0-1000	10	3.3333333
1000-2000	28	9.3333333
2000-3000	79	26.333333
3000-4000	65	21.666667
4000-5000	38	12.666667
5000-6000	20	6.6666667
6000-7000	10	3.3333333
7000-8000	13	4.3333333
8000-9000	5	1.6666667
9000-10000	16	5.3333333
10000-15000	7	2.3333333
15000-20000	2	0.6666667
20000-100000	7	2.3333333

Mean - 5733.00 Max. = 96000
S.D. = 8121.2145 Min. = 0

8121.21. The very high value of standard deviation shows that the variation of earning of individuals is very high. The 96 percent of the total population earn less than or equal to Rs. 12000 per year that is Rs. 1000 per month. This shows that most of the families are really poor.

Due to the less earning of the husband, wives also do some work and contribute to the family income as discussed earlier. The Table 5.2.2 presents the summarised data of frequency and percentage of wives earning per year. From the table we can see that nearly 36 percent women earn between Rs. 1500 to 2000 per year. The maximum earning of a woman has been noticed to be Rs. 13200.00 and that too, she was an Anganwadi Sevika that is a service class woman. The mean earning of women is Rs. 2133 with a standard deviation of Rs. 1556.50. It is clear that the earning of women is very less and their variation is also high. All the women are earning less than Rs. 1000.00 per month except one.

Table 5.2.2: Frequency distribution of Wife's Yearly Income (WYI)

Interval (Rs.)	*Frequency*	*Percent*
0-500	35	11.666667
500-1000	39	13
1000-1500	20	6.6666667
1500-2000	107	35.666667
2000-2500	13	4.3333333
2500-3000	58	19.333333
3000-3500	3	1
3500-4000	13	4.3333333
4000-6000	5	1.6666667
6000-8000	4	1.3333333
8000-10000	2	0.6666667
10000-15000	1	0.3333333

Mean = 2133.00 Max. = 13200
S.D. = 1556.4982 Min=0

Since, the earnings of husband as well as wives are low, therefore it is a general practice that children also work. Their earning has been summarised in Table 5.2.3. We can see from the table that nearly 70 percent children earn less than Rs. 1000 per year. This also includes the percentage of not working children. Also, the number of children earning between Rs. 1000/- to Rs. 2000/- and Rs. 2000/- to Rs. 3000/- per year are 29 and 30, respectively. Total 97 percent of children earn Rs. 6000/- per year that is Rs. 500/- per month. The average earning of the children is Rs. 1278.67 with a standard deviation of Rs.3356. This shows that per year income of the children is really very low and also there is high variation.

Table 5.2.3: Frequency distribution of Children's Yearly Income (CYI)

Interval (Rs.)	***Frequency***	***Percent***
0-1000	209	69.666667
1000-2000	29	9.6666667
2000-3000	30	10
3000-4000	11	3.6666667
4000-6000	12	4
6000-8000	4	1.3333333
8000-10000	3	1
10000-50000	2	0.6666667

Mean = 1278.6667 S.D. = 3355.9429
Max = 45000 Min = 0

Families also consist of some very close relatives like old father and mother, younger brother or sister, etc.. The earning of such family members have also been considered and presented in Table 5.2.4. We have seen that 77 percent of families have no such type of earning source. Total 15 families that is 5 percent have support of less than Rs. 1000 per year. The number of families having support of between Rs. 1000 to 2000 and Rs. 2000 to 3000 are 20 and 21, respectively. This makes, nearly 96 percent of families having support of less than Rs.3000 per year from such other sources. The average of such earning is Rs.631 per year.

Table 5.2.4: Frequency distribution of the yearly income of other close relatives like father, brother, etc. living in the same household (OYI)

Interval (Rs.)	*Frequency*	*Percent*
0	231	77
1-1000	15	5
1000-2000	20	6.6666667
2000-3000	21	7
3000-4000	6	2
4000-8000	6	2
8000-20000	1	0.333 3333

Mean = 631 Max. = 19000
S.D. = 1645.0206 Min. = 0

The total earning of each family can be obtained by adding the earnings of husband, wife, children and others and this has been presented in the tabular form in the Table 5.2.5. The total earning of 172 families that is 57.33 percent families lie between Rs. 5,000 to 10,000 per year. The number of families whose earning is between Rs. 1000 to 5,000 and Rs. 10,000 to 20,000 are 55 and 52 that is 18.33 percent and 17.33 percent, respectively. Hence, 94.3 percent families are having total earning of less than Rs. 20,000. The average per year earning per family is Rs. 9775.66 with a standard deviation of Rs.8936/-. We have also noticed that the minimum and maximum earning are of Rs. 700/- and Rs. 96,000/- per year respectively.

The correlation coefficient between all the four earnings have been calculated and presented in a

Table 5.2.5: Frequency distribution of Total yearly earning of the family

Interval (Rs.)	*Frequency*	*Percent*
700-1000	4	1.3333333
1000-5000	55	18.333333
5000-10000	172	57.333333
10000-20000	52	17.333333
20000-30000	7	2.3333333
30000-40000	3	1
40000-50000	4	1.3333333
> 50000	3	1

Mean = 9775.6667 Max. = 96000
S.D. = 8936.0179 Min. = 700

correlation matrix table (see Table 5.2.6). The value of correlation coefficient between husband's and wife's earning is positive but very small that is 0.06. Also, the correlation between the husband's earning and children's as well as others earning are negative and small that is –0.024 and –0.042, respectively. This means in a family as husband's income is high, the children's and other's income is low that is children and other members are not working, it is quite logical that if a person's income is sufficient then he won't send his children to work. Similarly, the correlation between wife's earning and children's earning is negative that is –0.05. This means that if in a family where females are also earning and their income is good enough then there is no need for children to go for work.

To study the nature of function between total earning and husband's earning as well as between total earning and wife's earning, we have defined the regression lines. Let T, H and W denote the total earning, husband's and wife's earning per year, respectively. The regression lines are

Table 5.2.6: Correlation Matrix of yearly income of husband, wife, children and other close relatives in the family

	HYI	*WYI*	*CY1*	*OYI*
HYI	1	0.062	–0.024	–0.042
WYI	0.062	1	–0.047	0.025
CYI	–0.024	–0.047	1	–0.116
OYI	–0.042	0.025	–0.116	1

$T = 4079841 - 0.994\ H$

and

$T = 7105.966 + 1.252\ W$

The above two lines of regression are the best fitted models with R^2 - 0.815 and 0.048, respectively. With the help of these two lines of regression, we can predict the total earning of a family if the husband's and wife's earnings are given.

The income model given by equation (5.1) has been fitted on the data of the Table 5.2.5. The estimated value of the parameters are K= 700 and α=0.966. The Chi square statistic has been calculated and, which yields p-value equal to 0.86×10^{-50}. This shows that the Pareto model of income is not an appropriate model for the total earning of the people of this region. In fact, this model provides a proper fit for larger income *i.e.,* total income is more than 5000 then the p-value is 0.05, but for the income below 5 thousand groups, this model gives very high expected frequencies whereas observed frequencies are very less and therefore the x^2 calculated becomes very high (=231.77, d.f. = 5) which yields a very small p-value. Thus, for the whole data, Pareto distribution of income cannot be considered as a probability model.

The information of domestic animals which is asked in question number 4 has been summarised in Table 5.3. Thirty-six percent that is 108 out of 300 respondents do not posses any domestic animals (see also Sr. No. 2 of Table 5.8). It can also be seen that one family possesses more than one type of domestic animals. From the table we can see that bullock is the most preferred pet animal and nearly 49 percent people have this, since approximately the same percent of population are involved in farming. The percentage of cows, goats and buffaloes are 25.33, 17.0 and 16.0, respectively. The pig as a domestic animal has been seen in only one family. The chickens are also kept as domestic animals in this region and their percentage is 12.33 percent.

Table 5.3: Frequency distribution of type of domestic animals they posses

Type	*Frequency*	*Percent*
No Animals	108	36
Cow	76	25.333333
Buffalo	48	16
Bullock	146	48.666667
Goat/sheeps	51	17
Chicken	37	12.333333
Pigs	1	0.3333333

The frequency distribution of the amount of total monthly expenditure is given in Table 5.4.1. The expenditures, the people of Melghat generally do on food (FDR), clothing (CF). Shelter (SE). Medicine (ME). Farming (FRE). animals (AE) and festivals (FTE) have been presented in Table 5.4.2. The percentage of number of families doing expenditures in different intervals are written in parenthesis. The statistics like minimum,

Table 5.4.1: Frequency distribution of monthly total expenditure

Interval (Rs.)	*Frequency*	*Percent*
0-300	23	7.6666667
300-600	160	53.333333
600-900	61	20.333333
900-1200	41	13.666667
1200-2100	14	4.6666667
2100-4000	1	0.3333333

Tabic 5.4.2: Frequency distribution of monthly expenditures on food (FI) K), clothing (CE), Shelter (SB), Medicine (ME), Farming (FRF), Animals (AE) and Festivals (FTE)

Heads interval	*FDE*		*CE*		*SE*		*IMF*		*FRF*		*AE*		*FTE*	
(Rs)		%		%		%		%		%		%		%
0-100	6	2.00	270	90.00	299	99.67	293	97.67	292	97.33	295	98.33	295	98.33
100-200	51	17.00	16	5.33	1	0.33	7	2.33	7	2.33	5	1.67	4	1.33
200-300	85	28.33	6	2.00	0	0.00	0	0.00	1	0.33	0	0.00	0	0.00
300-400	73	24.33	1	0.33	0	0.00	0	0.00	0	0.00	0	0.00	1	0.33
400-500	34	11.33	1	0.33	0	0.00	0	0.00	0	0.00	0	0.00	0	0.00
500-600	16	5.33	0	0.00	0	0.00	0	0.00	0	0.00	0	0.00	0	0.00
600-700	18	6.00	0	0.00	0	0.00	0	0.00	0	0.00	0	0.00	0	0.00
700-800	12	4.00	0	0.00	0	0.00	0	0.00	0	0.00	0	0.00	0	0.00
800-900	3	1.00	0	0.00	0	0.00	0	0.00	0	0.00	0	0.00	0	0.00
900-1000	2	0.67	1	0.33	0	0.00	0	0.00	0	0.00	0	0.00	0	0.00

maximum, mean and standard deviation of all the expenditures are given in Table 5.4.3.

Table 5.4.3: The minimum and maximum values, mean and standard deviation of monthly total expenditure, expenditures on food, clothing, shelter, medicine, farming, animals and festival

Heads	*Min.*	*Max.*	*Mean*	*S.D.*
MTE	50	4000	668.0667	358.8279
FDE	0	1000	389.5	181.9113
CE	0	1000	62.83	90.5777
SE	0	200	7.00	25.2281
ME	0	200	83.33	33.0535
FRF	0	300	51.33	52.9866
AE	0	200	27.16	44.0846
FTE	0	400	41.00	48.4095

The total monthly expenditures of 160 families *i.e.*, 53.33 percent families are making expenditure between Rs. 300 to 600 (see Table 5.4.1). From the same table, we can see that, spending between Rs. 600 to 900, between Rs. 900 to 1200, the percentage of families are 20.33 and 13.66, respectively. We can also observe that nearly 8 percent families are spending very meager amount *i.e.*, less than Rs. 300 and only one family is doing expenditure of Rs. 4000 per month. The average expenditure is of Rs. 668 per month with a standard deviation of Rs. 358.8.

From the Table 5.4.2, we find that the variation in expenditure between the families is on food only. Most of the families are spending less than Rs. 100, on the other heads like clothing (90 percent), shelter (99.66 percent), medicines (97.67 percent), farming (97.33 percent), animals (98.33 percent) and festivals (98.33 percent). The remaining persons are spending on all these heads between Rs. 100 to 200 per month except on clothing. In case of clothing, 6 persons have been seen, spending between Rs. 200 to 300 and one each between Rs. 300 to 400, Rs. 400 to 500 and Rs. 900 to 1000. The main variation in expenditure between the families is on food. A large number of persons are spending amount ranging from Rs. 100 to 500 on food (28.33 percent spend between Rs. 200 to 300, 24.33 percent spend between Rs. 300 to 400, 17.0 percent spend between Rs. 100 to 200 and 11.33 percent between Rs. 400 to 500). Limited numbers of persons are having expenditure above Rs. 600 and below Rs. 100. The average expenditure on food is Rs. 389.5 per month with a standard deviation of Rs. 181.9. Similarly, the average expenditure on clothing, shelter, medicine, farming, animals and festivals are 62.8, 7.0, 83.3, 51.3, 27.2 and 41.0, respectively (see Table 5.4.3). This means that the next three major expenditures after food are medicine, clothing and farming, respectively. Hence, we can see that in this region the people are facing various health problems and therefore they spend more money on medicines.

Table 5.5 provides the frequency distribution of different needs for which income is insufficient. Fifty-six percent of the population has informed that their income is insufficient for medicine, followed by 27 percent who informed that income is insufficient for clothes, whereas, 29.33 percent has not answered to these questions. A very few persons have answered about insufficiency of their income for repairing or building a new house. Before this question, in the question number 7 of the economic part of our questionnaire, it has been asked whether their income is sufficient for food and clothing. In response to this, 80.6 percent have answered that earning is sufficient for food and clothing (see S.N.4 of Table 5.8). In the

Table 5.5: Frequency distribution of different needs for which income is not sufficient

Needs	***Frequency***	***Percent***
NA	88	29.333333
Medicine	170	56.666667
Food	31	10.333333
Clothes	81	27
House repair	20	6.6666667
House building	8	2.6666667
Others	13	4.3333333

immediate next question *i.e.*, question number 8 when it has been asked that whether their earning satisfy all needs then 72.6 percent have replied 'No' (see S.N. 5 of Table 5.8). Hence, it is obvious that the people of Melghat region can fulfill the requirement of food and clothes only, from their earnings but it is difficult for them to fulfill all their other necessities.

Let Z denotes total monthly expenditure and X and Y denote expenditures on food and clothes per month, respectively. The models between total expenditure and food as well as total expenditure and clothes can be easily obtained by applying the method of least square as,

$$Z = 105.733 + 1.444\,X$$

and

$$Z = 560.003 - 1.720\,Y$$

Thus, the above two models provide an information that how the total month expenditure is being affected by food and clothes.

It will be quite interesting at this stage to know a model between total annual earning and total annual expenditure and *vice-versa*. Let TAI and TAE denote the total income and total expenditure per annum. The expenditures are considered as negative values and income as positive values.

The model which provides total income as a function of total expenditure is,

TAI = 1716.627–1.005 TAE

and the model which gives total expenditure as a function of total income is,

TAE = –5735.011 –0.233 TAI

The correlation coefficient between total annual earning and expenditure is 0.484 which shows that the correlation is positive *i.e.* as income is high, expenditure is also high.

The government is providing financial aid in this region to the needy. These aids are in different forms which have been discussed in the previous section. Serial number 6 of Table 5.8 reveals that 75 percent of the respondents have never received any government financial support. The 25 percent *i.e.,* 75 persons have received government grants and the detail of the different types of aids with number of recipients have been summarised in Table 5.6. From this table we can see that 23 persons have received the aid in the form of' Khauti, followed by 3.66 percent for agriculture. The other types of aids which are received by the people of this region are very few in number and they can be seen in Table 5.6 and they are Bamboo for hut, buffalo, bullocks, bullock-cart, chakki, cow, loan for education, farm, house, kirana -shop, latrine, medicine, well, water pump, seeds, taxi and tin as well as cash

Table 5.6: Frequency distribution of purpose of government grants received

Purpose	*Frequency*	*Percent*
Nil	225	75
Agriculture	11	3.6666667
Bamboo for hut	2	0.6666667
Buffalo	3	1
Bullocks	8	2.6666667
Bullock-cart	2	0.6666667
Cash	2	0.6666667
Chakki	1	0.3333333
Cow	1	0.3333333
Education	1	0.3333333
Farm	5	1.6666667
House	3	1
Khaoti	23	7.6666667
Kirana Shop	2	0.6666667
Latrine	3	1
Medicine	2	0.6666667
Pump	4	1.3333333
Seeds	2	0.6666667
Taxi	1	0.3333333
Tin	2	0.6666667
Well	5	1.6666667

support. The amount of financial aid has been given in Table 5.7. From this table we see that 75 percent of people are not getting any financial support as discussed earlier. Eight percent are getting financial support of less than Rs. 2000. Government has also provided financial support between Rs. 2000 to 4000, Rs.4000 to 6000, Rs. 6000 to 8000 and Rs.8000 to 10000 to 7, 16, 3 and 3 persons, respectively. Twenty-two persons that is 7.33 percent have been provided above Rs. 10.000. The maximum financial support is of Rs. 35,000 and the average financial support is of Rs. 2188.33 with standard deviation of Rs. 6069.53. It is clear here that only 25 percent persons have received financial support.

Table 5.7: Frequencies of amount of government grant

Amount (Rs.)	*Frequency*	*Percent*
0	225	75
1-2000	24	8
2000-4000	7	2.3333333
4000-6000	16	5.3333333
6000-8000	3	1
8000-10000	3	1
10000-15000	6	2
15000-20000	5	1.6666667
20000-25000	5	1.6666667
25000-30000	5	1.6666667
30000-35000	1	0.3333333

Mean = 2188.33 S.D. = 6069.5328
Max.-35000 Min. = 0

Table 5.8: Frequency distribution of the responses in 'yes' and 'no' in few different matters

Sl.no.	*Type*	*Response*			
		Yes	%	**No**	%
1	FDI	171	57.00	129	43.00
2	DA	192	64.00	108	36.00
3	DADI	72	24.00	228	76.00
4	FEFC	242	80.67	58	19.33
5	ESAN	82	27.33	218	72.67
6	GGA	75	25.00	225	75.00

FDI - Farm Dependent Income
DADI - Domestic Animal Dependent Income
ESAN - Earning Sufficient for All Needs
DA - Flaving Domestic Animals
EEFC - Earning Enough for Food and Clothing
GGA - Getting Government Aids

5.4. FINDINGS

From the analysis of economic data discussed in the previous section 5.3, we can conclude that the earning source of majority of people in the Melghat region is farming or labour in farms *i.e.,* agriculture based occupation is the main source of income in this region. To earn the livelihood, all the members of the family *i.e.,* husband, wife, children and other close relatives living in the same household work. The main contribution in the total earning is still of the husbands. Also, the total earning of the families are less. It is required to increase the productivity of the land by improving the technology and by providing irrigation facilities for agricultural development of this area. Apart from agricultural earning, the people posses domestic animals, and bullock is the most preferred pet animal as well as the existence of cows, goats and buffaloes are also common as pet animals.

The expenditures on daily needs are very less. The main item is their food on which they spend their money.

Caring Hut in the agriculture field (*Source* – Nayak, 2012)

House in Melghat

They also spend very little amount on their clothes, shelter, medicine, farming, animals and festivals, etc.. Most of them feel that their earning is insufficient to meet all their necessities whereas at the same time they feel that they earn sufficient for the requirement of food and clothes. The government is helping them to improve their economic status by providing different type of loans as well as food grains at the subsidized rates.

6

Analysis of Demographical Factors

6.1. INTRODUCTION

The study of human populations by statistical methods began in London in 1966, with the pioneering work of John Graunt. He analysed the only available data, lists of deaths classified by cause, and he attempted, to assess the average size of families and households, the extent of migratory movements, and other elements of population structure and change. Late, in the seventeenth century, Edmund Hallay the astronomer, examined the Church records of Breslau and added the number of deaths at various ages to construct a life table. During the eighteenth century, statistics of this kind were assembled elsewhere and improved analysis was made, notably by Richard Price, leading to the development of life assurance. Later, there was much discussion of population philosophies - speculation about the likely effects of population growth on general prosperity. These early advances illustrate some of the main characteristics of Demography (see Cox, 1970; 1976; Pande, 1989a).

The area of demography in Statistics is defined as the quantitative study of human populations. Specific topics directly within the field of demography are fertility, migration, mortality, nuptiality, etc.. The basic materials used for its study are censuses, vital statistics and, increasingly, sample surveys. Its central concerns are the measurement and discovery of uniformities in the basic processes of human birth, death, population movement and population growth. The methods of demography are empirical and statistical and make as much use of advanced mathematics. Like anthropology and psychology, demography bridges the social and biological sciences (Spengler and Duncan, 1963); Hansraj, 1989); Pressat, 1973), etc.).

A distinction is commonly made between "formal" or "pure", demography and broader population studies. Formal demography is a well defined, technical subject with a highly developed mathematical methodology. It is concerned primarily with population structure that is, the age, sex, and marital composition of the population as it contributes to the understanding of population change. Formal demography has provided some of the most fruitful uses of mathematical models in the social sciences (see also, Ghosh, 1978).

A broader and increasingly popular usage of the term demography includes studies of demographic variables in their social contexts as well as their biological contexts (see Spengler and Duncan, 1963). In this approach, demographic changes are viewed as part of, and as both cause and effect of their social environment. Demographic analysis has also come to mean "not only the statistical manipulation of population data but more importantly, the study of such data as a method of solving empirical problems" (see Spengler and Duncan, 1956). In addition to the components of population change, demographic variables are rather arbitrarily assumed to include those mass measurements of population that are commonly enumerated in population censuses (see Thompson and Lewis, 1950).

The broader definition of demography inevitably involves inter-disciplinary aspects, since demographers and pure statisticians may study human populations in relation to other variables. Beyond the specific discipline of formal demography there is no distinguishing criterion of demography as such, other than its involvement in quantitative measures of human population. Thus, it can be said that the subject matter of demography includes those population theories that are based on quantitative observation and generalization. There is no firm line of demarcation, nor should one be expected.

Categories of Demography

Demographic studies can be placed broadly under four categories, namely descriptive demography under which census and registration statistics are studied. Then, comes analytical demography which deals with analysis and rates and ratios of the data collected. Third category is the comparative demography under which the study of different aspects at two different places and at two different points of time is covered. The fourth and last category is the historical category under which time series rates are studied (for details, see Hansraj, 1996).

Advantages of Demographic Studies

All over the world, population has been rapidly increasing and the same trend has been seen in India too. But merely saying that it has been increasing does not serve much purpose as well as does not provide any numerical evidence. It is with the help of serious study of demography or population problems that one would come to know about the extent of increase in population and also about the responsibility of the state and citizens in respect of social, economic and political problems of people as well as the state and their possible solutions as well. The important advantages of the study of demography may briefly be discussed as under.

1) Political

In the political field on the basis of demographic studies concerned political leadership and authorities come to know about the rate at which number of voters, male and female, is increasing, how the generation gap is gradually influencing national and international politics, which are the pockets of new concentration where more stress should be laid, what type of arrangements will be needed for conducting elections, which are the areas from where population is migrating and constituencies delimited accordingly so that there are no dummy or semi-dummy constituencies.

2) Economy

The importance of study of demography in the economic field is immense. It is with the help of these studies that the nation comes to know how far the rate of population growth is keeping pace with that of economic development and in case both are not keeping pace with each other, how to adjust these so that economic problems do not seriously threat the nation. Obviously, if the population growth rate is faster than economic growth rate then there will be economic crises, poverty and shortages. The problem will have to be solved either by solving population growth rate or by speeding of economic development plans. It is again demographic study which provides information about per capita income of the people, their consumption habits, per capita production and consumption rate, etc..

3) Planning

Most of the advanced countries are implementing the concept of planned development. Our country too has a planned system of development in the form of 5 year plans. Thus, the planning of resources has become an unavoidable process. It is expected that limited human and natural resources must be utilized in a planned manner in the best interest of the society. But, no planning can be a success unless the planners are aware of the population growth rate and the areas in which population is much more rapidly growing than the others. It is with the help of demographic studies that the planners can allocate resources to avoid regional imbalances and also provide for more mouths to be fed in the coming years. Also, it is with the help of these studies and demographic data that it becomes possible for the planners to provide for more educational institutions, hospitals, transport and essential services and to ensure that the people, whether the number is increasing or decreasing, get what is essentially needed by them.

4) Social

It is demographic studies which can help in finding out extra electricity, road, water, housing, schools, hospitals and other similar needs of the society on one hand and shopping centres, hygienic facilities, etc. on the other (see Heer, 1978). Again, it is with the help of these studies that the state can come to know about the magnitude of law and order problems, which growing population will create and how to solve these problems so that the citizens feel secure. Even developed countries are trying to provide social security to the population by providing old age pension, health insurance, child care and maternity centres and so on. These steps can effectively be taken with the help of demographic studies only.

5) Advantages to administrators

Demographic studies help the administrators to understand where there should be more and where less stress on administration. In fact, whole administrative machinery moves by keeping in view the growth of population. An administrator, whether in the social, economic or political field will always take the growth or decline of population in view for a smooth running of administration?

6) Checking regional imbalances

Demographic study is essential for finding out population migration trends which result in creating regional imbalances, particularly when due to one reason or the other there is mass migration. This trend is quite visible these days because the educated people and landless labour is migrating from rural to the urban areas and from one region to the other. Many serious law and order problems arise because of it and even some regions become more advanced industrially than the other, thus creating industrial backwardness in some parts of the country.

6.2. FACTORS UNDER CONSIDERATION

To study the demographical characteristics, several factors have been considered in the present work and the data related to these have been collected and analysed (see also, Sinha, 1986). These factors have been discussed here in brief.

Marriage and Fertility

Marriage is of interest to demographers mainly because of its influence on fertility (Basil, 1993a). Comparative analysis is complicated by the differing nature of the marriage bond and the degree of ease with which marriages can be ended in various parts of the world. The most significant feature is the age at which marriages take place. The age at which the girls get married depend on social values. This also decides the number of children a couple produces as well as the length of time of having first child from marriage. An inappropriate age of marriage sometimes can be fatal during pregnancy) or delivery for mother as well as child. This affects the death of children. Apart from this, the other factors which affect mortality are the place of delivery and presence of doctor or nurse.

Hospital Facility

If the hospital or primary health centre are not in the village or far away from the village, such situations arc dangerous for mother and child. If mobile hospital is visiting the villages then this facility must be frequent and regular. All the above factors directly affect the death of children in this area and therefore their study is must.

Family Planning Programme

Family welfare program impact on the society is very less in this region. Since, the people do not know about the family planning, they produce more children without proper spacing. This may increase the mortality of mother and children. Therefore, it becomes necessary to assess the different aspects of family planning programs in this region. It is important here to collect the information about their opinion regarding necessity of family planning, their knowledge of family planning, knowledge about using the family planning methods, etc.. Here, it is also important to search out, whether the most commonly practiced family planning method is male based or female based. On the other hand, it is a common practice that the people are not aware and not interested in different family planning programs, but they are being forced by government officials to implement it just to complete the target of pre-decided government's number of cases. It has also been seen in our collected data in a few cases that husband and wife both were operated by officials for family planning. Sometimes, due to their illiteracy they may not get correct information about family planning therefore it also becomes important to study their source of information.

Vaccination of Children

As pointed earlier the deaths of children are high in Melghat region and this can be prevented also by implementing the vaccination program properly (cf. also, Chand, 1994). The government is taking a lot of efforts in this direction but still it is not clear that whether the program is reaching upto the interior villages of Melghat region. To assess this, some questions related to vaccination has also been asked. The point of stress are the source of treatment for any disease, opinions regarding vaccination of children, opinions about benefit of vaccination, number of children vaccinated, number of vaccines given to children, diseases for which vaccines arc given and places of vaccination. The aim of considering these factors is to explore their attitude towards child care.

Dietary Habits

The health and nutrition problems of the population in this region are varied. The nutritional problems of different communities located at various stages of development are full of insecurities and very little scientific information on dietary habits and nutrition status are available due to lack of systematic and comprehensive research investigations. Malnutrition is common and greatly affects the ability to resists infection, leading to chronic illness and in the post weaning period, leading to death (Basu, 1993b). The situation is particularly serious in view of the fact that the women even during their pregnancy have a heavy work load. Maternal and child malnutrition are common in this region. Also, the nutritional status of pregnant women directly influences their reproductive performance and the birth is crucial to infants' chances of survival and to its subsequent growth and development. Nutrition also affects lactation and breast feeding which are key elements in the health of infants and young children. To study the dietary habits as well as malnutritional status of children, the factors like food habits, status of vegetarian or non-vegetarian, availability of two full meals per day, number of non-vegetarian meals per week and types of non-veg have been considered for this present work (see Basu, 1990).

Child Feeding Habits

Similarly, to study the specific malnutritional status of children, the factors such as breast feeding habits, the duration of breast feeding, supplementary food, age of starting supplementary foods and the food grains used for preparing the supplementary foods are also needed to be analysed. Also, it may be quite informative to know the awareness about giving the medicines to children. The questions can be asked about their opinion, for giving medicines to children as well as, whether they go themselves for vaccines, medicines, etc. to the hospitals.

Demographic Parameters

The information of the total population of children in the age-group of 0-5 years can highlight the status of children in this region. This can be done by estimating the total population of the children in the age group of 0-5 years and estimated crude birth rate with the help of gathered data. Let, x denotes the average number of children in a house and V denotes the total number of households in this region. The estimated total population of children can be obtained as,

$$C = V.\, x$$

Where, C denotes the estimate of total population of children between the age-group of 0-5 years.

Also, the crude birth rate (CBR) can be obtained by using the formula.

$$\text{CBR} = \frac{\text{Total number of live births which occurred in the given region during the given period}}{\text{Total population in the given region during the given period}} \times 1000 \qquad ***(6.1)$$

Similarly, the information about total number of deaths can give an idea about the deaths of children in this region. This can be done by calculating the estimated number of deaths during the last five years and calculating the infant mortality rate (IMR) (cf. Parsuraman and Rajan, 1990). Let, $\bar{y}$ denote the average deaths of children between the age-group of 0-5 years in a house-hold and V denotes the number of households, then

$$D = \bar{y} \,.\, V$$

Where, D is the estimated deaths of children between the age-group of 0-5 years per year. The foetal death rate (FDR), the age specific death rate (ASDR) and infant mortality rate (IMR) can be calculated by using the following formula.

$$\text{FDR (Still- birth)} = \frac{\text{Total number of foetal deaths}}{\text{Total number of live births during the given period}} \times 1000 \qquad ***(6.2)$$

$$\text{ASDR} = \frac{\text{Number of deaths in a specific age group,}}{\text{Total population}} \times 1000 \qquad ***(6\ 3)$$

and

$$\text{IMR} = \frac{\text{Number of children who die before completing 1 year of their life}}{\text{Number of children live in the same vear}} \times 1000 \qquad ***(6.4)$$

The number of households in the Melghat region is approximately 40,000 as discussed in chapter 2, section 3. Also, the total population of 300 families which have been considered in our sample is 1667 (see Table 4.10). With the help of these two information, the average number of family members and the total population of 40,000 households *i.e.,* the population of Melghat region can be estimated and the estimated population is 2, 22, 267 approximately. Now, considering the value of total population and the number of house-holds as well as calculating crude birth rate, still birth rate, age specific death rate and infant mortality rate, inference can be drawn about mortality of children in Melghat region.

6.3. MODELS

Model for Gap Before Having First Child from Marriage

Let 'X' denotes the time interval between marriage and first child. To define the probability density function for X, a linear combination of Binomial and Exponential distribution can be thought of. Let X follows Exponential distribution, then its probability density function (p.d.f), is given by -

$$f_e(X) = \theta\, e^{-\theta x}\ ;\ X > 0,\ \theta > 0 \qquad ***\ (6.5)$$

and cumulative distribution function (c.d.f.) of (6.5) is defined as.

$$F_e(x) = 1 - e^{-\theta x} \qquad *** (6.6)$$

Also, the p.d.f and c.d.f. of Binomial distribution are given by equation (4.1) and (4.2), respectively. A convex combination of equation (6.5) and (4.1) can be defined as.

$$f^P(X) = c\, f_e(X) + (1\text{-}c).\ p_B(X),\ 0 \leq c \geq 1 \qquad *** (6.7)$$

This p.d.f. is a mixture of continuous and discrete distributions, which gives a probability p' at point x, since at that point the probability density function, f_e (X) will be 0, due to being a continuous function. The c.d.f of the proposed distribution $f^P(X)$ is

$$F^p(x) = c\, F_e(x) + (1\text{-}c)\ .\ F_B(x) \qquad *** (6.8)$$

For different values of x, the F^p (x) can be calculated and with the help of these probabilities, the expected frequencies can be obtained. The unknown parameters can be estimated by using maximum likelihood estimator method (MLE) and/or any suitable numerical iteration method.

Model for the births in last five years

Let 'X' be the number of births during the last 5 years, *i.e.*, X can take any value from 0 to 5, the model for X can be suggested as Binomial distribution which has already been defined by equation (4.1) and (4.2) in Chapter 4.

The values of unknown parameters n and p can be estimated from the data and goodness of fit test can be conducted.

Model for the deaths in the last five years

Let 'X' denotes the number of deaths that occurred in a family during the last 5 years, the model for this will follow a Binomial distribution which is defined by equation (4.1). It is also evident that the number of deaths X decreases exponentially in case of children. Therefore, in this case also, a linear combination of Binomial and Exponential distribution which is defined by equation (6.7) can be suggested.

6.4. ANALYSIS OF DEMOGRAPHICAL DATA

The data collected regarding demographical factors as per part 3 of the questionnaire, enclosed in appendix "A", has been analysed in this section. The related theory has already been presented in brief in the previous sub-sections. The data of demographical variables have been summarized and presented in the tabular form from Table 6.1.1 to Table 6.8.2.

The Table 6.1.1 gives frequency distribution of the age at the time of marriage of female and length of time before having the first child, from marriage. From this table we can see that the number of persons who have not replied about their age at the time of marriage and the duration before having first child are 38 and 46 respectively. It can also be seen that the maximum marriages have taken place in the age group of 18 to 20 years. Marriages at a very young age are not rare. Marriages have also taken place before 18 years of age. *i.e.,* as young as 14 to 18 years, but this percentage is comparatively low. Similarly, marriages are observed upto the age of 25 years, but as age increases above 20 years the percentage of number of marriages decreases.

It can also be seen from this table that maximum number of females has given birth to a child after one

Table 6.1.1: Frequency distribution of age at marriage and spacing before first child from marriage spacing (in years)

Age at marriage	*NA*	*1*	*2*	*3*	*4*	*Total*	*Percent*
NA	37	1	0	0	0	38.00	12.67
14	1	1	1	1	0	4.00	1.33
15	0	0	2	4	0	6.00	2.00
16	0	^	1	0	0	4.00	1.33
17	0	6	11	–	0	19.00	6.33
18	0	35	27	4	0	66.00	22.00
19	o	21	14	–	1	38.00	12.7
20	3	31	17	1	0	52.00	17.3
21	1	12	11	1	0	25.00	8.3
22	0	18	–	0	0	21.00	7.0
23	0	8	4	0	0	12.00	4.0
24	3	4	5	0	0	9.00	3.0
25	1	2	1	1	1	6.00	1.9
Total	46	142	94	16	2		
Percent	15.33	47.33	31.33	5.33	0.667		

year of marriage *i.e.,* 47.3 percent. Total 94 females *i.e.,* 31.3 percent have given birth to a child after 2 years of marriage. The percentage of females who have delivered their first child after 3 and 4 years of marriage are 5.3 and 0.7 percent, respectively and these percentages are quite low. Since marriages are being done at a very young age and in most of the cases, the birth of the first child is taking place after 1 year of marriage and, therefore, female get a large span of child bearing age. Hence, they will produce more number of children unless they take some family planning measures.

The frequency distribution of the place of delivery has been presented in Table 6.1.2. Here, it can be seen that most of the delivery *i.e.,* nearly 84 percent are taking place

Table 6.1.2: Frequency distribution of the place of delivery

Place	*Frequency*	*Percent*
Na	31	10.3
At home	253	84 3
Government hospitals	8	2.67
Primarv health centre	8	2.67

Table 6.1.3: Frequency distribution of the presence of nurses during delivery

	Frequency	*Percent*
Na	31	10.3
N	45	15
Y	224	74.7

Table 6.1.4: Frequency distribution of who did the delivery

	Frequency	*Percent*
Na	31	10.3
Mother and other ladies	59	19 7
Neighbouring ladies	25	8.33
Nurse	180	60.0
Other	5	1.67

at home. The percentage of deliveries in government hospital or primary health centers are very less *i.e.,* 2.7 percent for each. Since, a very significant number of children are taking birth at home without appropriate facilities; this may be one of the causes of high death rate of children in this region.

From 6.1.4, we can see that most of the deliveries *i.e.,* 60.0 percent are taking place in presence of a nurse though that takes place at home. In reply of the previous question (see Table 6.1.3), nearly 75 percent have responded that nurses are present during the delivery time and only 15 percent answered about the absence of nurses. It has also been seen that some of the deliveries are being done by mother and other ladies at home (*i.e.,* 19.7 percent) as well as neighboring ladies (*i.e.,* 8.3 percent).

In the next Table 6.2.1, their responses regarding the hospital primary health centre facility in their village, has been summarized. Here, they have been asked about the presence of a hospital in near their village. In response to this, 87.4 percent have answered positively and informed about the presence of a hospital in near their village. Whereas, 12.3 percent have given negative response about its presence and only 1 person has not answered the question. It seems that most of the people have the hospital primary health facility.

It can be seen from the Table 6.2.2, that the mobile hospital facility provided by government, also visits their villages. Here, 66.66 percent *i.e.,* 200 people have said that the mobile hospital visits their village once in a week. Fifty one people out of 300 *i.e.,* 17 percent have answered that it visits their village twice in a week. Nearly equal number of people *i.e.,* 16 percent has informed about more number of visits per week of this hospital to their village and 1 person has not answered this question.

The Table 6.2.3 gives the frequency distribution of the number of times a particular respondent visits a hospital. It is evident from this table that most of the people *i.e.,* 93 percent go to a hospital only when they feel necessary. Also, 3.7 percent people have informed that they visit the hospital once in a month. Two persons each out of 300 have reported about their visit to the hospital once in a week and once in a fortnight.

Table 6.2.1: Frequency distribution of hospital near village

	Frequency	*Percent*
Na	1	0.33
N	37	12.3
Y	262	87.4

Table 6.2.2: Frequency distribution of number of visits of a mobile hospital in a village

	Frequency	*Percent*
Na	1	0.33
Once in a week	200	66.7
Twice in a week	51	17
More number of times	48	16

Table 6.2.3: Frequency distribution of number of visits to a hospital

	Frequency	*Percent*
Na	6	2
Once in a week	2	0.67
Once in 15 days	2	0.67
Once in a month	11	3.67
Whenever necessary	279	93

Family planning plays a crucial role in controlling the population of a society. The different aspects of family planning have been asked from the respondents and their responses which are in the form of' 'Yes' or 'No' have been summarized in Table 6.3.1. Here, it can be seen that 205 respondents *i.e.,* 68.3 percent have the knowledge of family planning and 29.7 percent respondents do not have this knowledge. When the necessity of the family planning has been asked to the respondents then 46.7 percent have said that they think it is necessary and only 4.3 percent find, it is unnecessary. A large number of respondents *i.e.,* 147

Table 6.3.1: Responses regarding family planning program

	Yes		***No***		***NA***	
		%		%		%
Knowledge of family planning	205	68.3	89	29.7	6	2.0
Necessity of family planning	140	46.7	13	4.3	147	49.0
Information about different methods of F.P.	97	32.3	162	54.0	41	13.7
Using any family planning method	96	32.0	74	24.7	130	43.3
Using male family planning method	34	11.3	38	12.7	228	76.0
Using female family planning method	39	13.0	JJ	11.0	228	76.0
Easy availability of these things	76	25.3	39	13.0	185	61.7
These things available free of cost	78	26.0	35	11.7	187	62.3
Knowledge of using these things	45	15.0	62	20.7	193	64.3

have not answered this critical question. The knowledge of family planning methods is not very high in this region. Fifty-four percent people do not have any information about different methods of family planning where as 32.3 percent have knowledge of it.

A large number of people *i.e.,* 43.3 percent have not answered the question when asked about using any family planning method. Out of 300, only 96 *i.e.,* 32 percent have informed about currently using family planning methods and 24.7 percent are not using it. It is also seen that, 11.3 percent are using male family planning methods and 13 percent are using female family planning methods whereas 76 percent people have avoided answering these questions. It means family planning methods are still not being used by a large segment of the population in this region. The question has also been asked about the easy availability of the necessary materials needed for family planning. In response to this, 25.3 percent respondents have said that it is easily available and 13 percent have reported about the non-availability of these things. As government provides the necessary facilities of family planning, free of cost but here, only 26 percent have informed about the availability of these things, free of cost and 11.7 percent have said that they purchase such things from the market. The knowledge of using family planning methods are lacking in this region. Only 15 percent have said that they have the knowledge of using these materials whereas 20.7 percent reported about not having the knowledge of using it. It is important here to note that a very large number of respondents *i.e.,* above 61 percent have avoided answering the above discussed three questions, may be due to illiteracy and shyness.

Table 6.3.2 provides the summarized data of the different sources of getting information about family planning. The maximum number of people *i.e.,* 95 has not answered the question. Ninety two *i.e.,* 30.7 percent have got this information from Anganwadi, whereas 26.7 percent from other sources such as media, newspaper, friends, etc.. A very few people are getting the information from gram sevak sevika and gram panchayat. Their percentages are 5.7 and 5.3 respectively. Thus, gram

Table 6.3.2: Frequency distribution of the different sources of information about family planning

	Frequency	***Percent***
No. information	95	31.7
Gram Sevak/sevika	17	5.67
Gram panchayat	16	5.3
Anganwadi	92	30.7
Other sources	80	26.7

sevak/sevika are not spreading the information related to the family planning methods to the people as expected.

The data collected regarding the number of children in each family is given in Table 6.4.1. Here, it is found that the maximum numbers of families have 3 children and their percentage is 34.7. The percentages of families having 4 and 5 children are 16.3 and 10.3, respectively. Whereas, the percentages of 1 and 2 children are 10.7 and 15.7 respectively, but these couples were still in child bearing age-group and producing more children may not be ruled out. The average children per family are 3.1 on the basis of collected data.

Table 6.4.1: Frequency distribution of number of children in the family

	Frequency	***Percent***
NA	30	10
1	32	10.7
2	47	15.7
3	104	34.7
4	49	16.3
5	31	10.3
6	4	1.33
7	1	0.33
8	2	0.67

Total children = 836; Mean = 3.10

In the Table 6.4.2, the frequency distributions of the different sources from which the people take treatment are given. We can see that, the maximum people *i.e.,* 75.66 percent take treatment from the primary health center nearest to their village. The government mobile hospital also provides treatment to the people and their percentage is 48. These two are the main providers of the treatment

Table 6.4.2: Frequency distribution of source of treatment

	Frequency	*Percent*
NA	2	0.67
Home remedies	5	1.67
Mantrik	3	1
Govt. Mobile Hospital	144	48
Primary H.C.	227	75.7
Vaidh	7	2:33

facility, whereas the treatment from Vaidh, Mantrik and home remedies are nearly negligible. Here, it is to be noted that the treatment of Mantriks are still in existence in this region.

In Table 6.4.3, the replies of respondents about the vaccination of children are given. We can see that 96.3 percent people have vaccinated their children and only 1.33 percent have not vaccinated. Similarly, nearly 98 percent people have vaccinated to all the children in their family. Only 2 families have not vaccinated all the children in their family. This shows that the people are aware of vaccination as well as they do vaccinate their children. Surprisingly, only 47 percent people feel that their child is protected against the diseases after vaccination,

Table 6.4.3: The reply of respondents regarding vaccination of children

	Yes	*%*	*No*	*%*	*NA*	*%*
Knowledge of family planning	205	68.3	89	29.7	6	2.0
Vaccinated children	289	96.3	7	1.3	7	2.33
All the children in family vaccinated	293	97.7	2	0.7	5	1.67
After vaccination child is protected against diseases	141	47.0	156	52.0	3	1
No vaccination can lead to death	104	34.7	190	63.3	6	2

whereas 52 percent did not feel this. Similarly, a large number of people *i.e.,* 63.3 percent think that without vaccination their children cannot die and 34.7 percent feel that their children can die without vaccination.

Above, we have seen that generally the people are aware about the vaccination but it is also important to know- whether they give all types of vaccines to their children as suggested by health officials. The information regarding the number of vaccines given to the children are presented in the Table 6.4.4. The maximum numbers of people *i.e.,* 44 percent have given only one vaccine and nearly equal *i.e.,* 43 percent have given 2 vaccines. The percentages of people who have given 3 or more vaccines are very less *i.e.,* nearly 3 percent for three and four vaccines. Whereas, 6 vaccines have been given by only one family and 5 vaccines have given by 3 families.

Table 6.4.4: Frequency distribution of number of vaccines given

	Frequency	***Percent***
NA	17	5.67
1	132	44
2	129	43
3	8	2.67
4	10	3.33
5	3	1
6	1	0.33

Mean = 1.58 S. D. = 0.89

The Table 6.4.5 gives the frequency distribution of the vaccines given for various diseases. It has been seen that the maximum people *i.e.,* 86.66 percent have given triple + polio vaccine to their children. Then, 43.66 percent have given the BCG vaccines. The vaccines for pox and measles have been given to children of only 1 and 3 families,

Table 6.4.5: Frequency distribution of vaccines of different diseases.

	Frequency	*Percent*
NA	17	5.67
BCG	131	43.7
Triple + polio	260	86.7
Pox	1	0.33
Measles	3	1
Manengitis	0	0

respectively. Whereas, no family has given the meningitis vaccine to their children. Here, we can conclude that the government program of triple polio is reaching upto the people in this region.

The next Table provides the information about the places where the child is vaccinated. From the Table 6.4.6, it is clear that 57 percent *i.e.,* maximum number of people vaccinate their children from government mobile hospital and 29.7 percent from primary health centers. These two are the main centres where most of the people (nearly 87 percent) do the vaccination to their children. Private Doctors also provide vaccines but their contribution in this area is very less *i.e.,* 2 percent only.

Table 6.4.6: Frequency distribution of place where the child is vaccinated

	Frequency	*Percent*
NA	9	3
Govt. Mobile hospital	171	57
Primary health centre	89	29.7
Private doctor	6	2
Social worker	0	0
Others	25	8.33

The food habits of the people of this region are given in the Table 6.5.1, this table shows that nearly 67 percent of the total population takes mixed diet *i.e.,* vegetarian and non-vegetarian both. The percentages of purely vegetarian and non-vegetarian persons are nearly equal and their percentages are 16.3 and 17, respectively. Similarly, the response regarding the availability of two full meals per day has been gathered to know the malnutrition status, 95.3 percent people have said that they get two full meals everyday and 4.7 percent have said, they do not get it (see Table 6.5.2). The number of times, the people of Melghat region eat non-vegetarian meals per week has also been asked to assess their intake of highly nutritious diet which is summarized in Table 6.5.3. We can observe that 84.3 percent take it whenever it is possible for them. Also, every days as well as, upto 5 times in a week are nearly impossible to take such meals

Table 6.5.1: Frequency distribution of different food habits

	Frequency	***Percent***
Vegetarian	49	16.3
Non - veg	51	17
Mixed diet	200	66.7

Table 6.5.2: Frequencies of the responses about the availability of two full meals per day

	Frequency	***Percent***
Y	286	95.3
N	14	4.67

Table 6.5.3: Frequency distribution of number of non-veg meals

	Frequency	***Percent***
NA	44	14.7
Everyday	2	0.67
5 times in a week	1	0.33
Whenever possible	253	84.3

for them. It means they take it rarely. The Table 6.5.4 gives the frequency distribution of different types of non-veg by which they prepare their meals. Chickens are the most popular non-veg (79.33 percent people eat it). And the next popular is goats (59.33 percent people eat it). The fish and birds are also being eaten in this region and their percentages are 21.66 and 11.66 respectively, whereas we have seen only two families who eat pigs.

Table 6.5.4: Frequency distribution of different types of non-veg foods

	Frequency	*Percent*
NA	44	14.7
Birds	35	11.7
Goats	178	59.3
Pigs	2	0.67
Chicken	238	79.93
Fishes	65	21.7

Since, malnutrition is common in children of this region, therefore the question has been asked about breast feeding practices, duration of breast feeding and supplementary food, etc. and this information is summarized in the Tables 6.6.1 to 6.6.4. It can be seen from Table 6.6.1 that nearly 90 percent mothers give breast feeding to their children. Similarly, 88.3 percent give supplementary foods other than breast feeding to their children. The numbers of cases who do not breast

Table 6.6.1: Response regarding breast feeding and supplementary food

	Yes	%	*No*	%	*NA*	%
Breast feeding to children	269	90	2	0.7	29	9.67
Giving supplementary food other than breast feeding	265	88	3	1	32	10.7

feed, and do not give supplementary food other than breast feeding are very limited (2 and 3 respectively). From Table 6.6.2, we observe that all the mothers provide breast feeding to their children for more than 3 months, since no family has been seen who give breast feeding upto 3 months. The 44.7 percent people give breast feeding upto 9 months of age and 40.3 percent give upto 12 months of age. That is more than 40 percent mothers are giving breast feeding to their child for either nine months or 12 months. Only one family has answered that they breast feed their children upto 6 months only and two families have been seen who breast fed upto the birth of next child. Such type of cases is rare. In addition to the breast feeding, they also give some supplementary foods to their children (see Table 6.6.3). It is seen that 144 people *i.e.,* 48 percent are giving supplementary foods from the age of 8 months and 111 people *i.e.,* 37 percent from the age of 6 months. At the very young age *i.e.,* upto 4 months of age and above 8 months of age, two families have been observed who start giving supplementary foods to their children. Hence, it can be concluded that between the ages of 6 to 8 months people start giving supplementary foods. In Table 6.6.4, the frequency distribution of the grains from which the supplementary food is prepared has been given. It can be

Table 6.6.2: Frequency distribution of number of months upto for which breast feeding is given to children

	Frequency	***Percentage***
NA	42	14
3 Months	0	0
6 Months	1	0.33
9 Months	134	44.7
12 Months	121	40.3
Till the birth of next child	2	0.67

Table 6.6.3: Frequency distribution of age (in months) from which supple-mentary food is given to children

	Frequency	***Percent***
NA	41	13.7
2 Months of age	0	0
4 Months of age	2	0.67
6 Months of age	111	37
8 Months of age	144	48
Above 8 months of age	2	0.67

Mean = 3.08 S.D. = 1.32

Table 6.6.4: Frequency distribution of food grains from which this supple-mentary food is prepared

	Frequency	***Percent***
NA	34	11.3
Rice	158	52.7
Jowar	198	66
Bajra	14	4.67
Dal	39	13
Anganvadi food	108	36

observed that 198 people *i.e.,* 66 percent prepare the supplementary food from Jowar, 158 people *i.e.,* 52.66 percent from Rice and 108 people *i.e.,* 36 percent give their children the food provided by Anganwadi. Also, 39 people *i.e.,* 13 percent prepare their food from Dal and 14 people *i.e.,* 4.66 percent prepare from Bajra. Hence, it can be concluded that the people prepare the supplementary food using Rice, Jowar, Bajra, Dal but the use of Jowar and Rice is very high.

The Table 6.7 gives the opinion of respondents regarding awareness of providing medicines to their children and their attitude about going to the hospital themselves for vaccinations, medicines, etc.. We can see

Table 6.7: Responses regarding awareness of providing medicine to children

	Yes	*No*	*NA*
Giving medicines to children for not falling ill	288 (96.0)	1 (0.3)	11 (3.7)
Going to hospital on his own for injections, medicines or vaccination	172 (57.3)	123 (41.0)	5 (1.7)

(Values in parenthesis are the percentages)

that 96 percent of the total respondents give medicines to their children for not getting sick. That is, most of the people are aware about medicines. To give medicines to their children, 57.3 percent people go to the hospital on their own whereas 41 percent do not go.

The numbers of children born in last five years, of the respondent's families are given in Table 6.8.1. It is clear that 2 percent families have produced 4 children in the duration of 5 years. Also, the percentage of families who have given birth to 3.2 and 1 child are 6.7, 20.0 and 24.3, respectively. Thus, 277 children have taken birth in 300 families in the last 5 years. And hence the estimated birth of the children in last 5 years is 36.933 in Melghat region. This is the estimated size of population in the age-group of 0-5 years (= c). This implies that there are approximately

Table 6.8.1: Frequency distribution of number of children born in last 5 years in the families

	Frequency	*Percent*
NA	141	47
1	73	24.3
2	60	20
3	20	6.67
4	6	2
5	0	0

7387 live births in one year *i.e.,* during last year. The Crude Birth Rate (CBR) can be calculated with the help of the value of total live births in one year and total population, using equation (6.1), which comes out to be 33.23. It is important to note here that this CBR is much higher than CBR of rural Maharashtra which is 21.6 as well as Rural India which is 27.6 (see for details, Report of National Commission on Population, Govt. of India (2001).

The number of deaths that have occurred during the last five years of different ages, from 1 to 5 years as well as still births are given in Table 6.8.2. The table shows that as age increases the percentage of deaths decreases. The percentage of still births is maximum *i.e.,* 9 percent. We can see that total 43 deaths have occurred except still births during last 5 years in the families of 300 respondents. This gives the total 5733 deaths in 5 years *i.e.,* approximately 1147 (= D) children of 0 - 5 years age-group per year. It can also be seen that 7.6 percent have died within 1 year, 3.0 percent within two years, 1.7 percent within 3 years and 0.67 percent within 5 years of age. The still birth rate defined in equation (6.2) is calculated to be 97.46. Now, the age specific *i.e.,* between 0 to 5 years death rate as defined in equation (6.3) can be

Table 6.8.2: Frequency distribution of number of child deaths in the families in last 5 years according to their ages

	Frequency	***Percent***
Still Birth	27	9
1 year	23	7.67
2 year	9	3
3 year	5	1.67
4 year	4	1.33
5 year	2	0.67

calculated, which are 5.16. Similarly, the infant mortality rate (1MR), defined in equation (6.4) can be calculated which is 82.98 whereas the estimated death of infants in a year in the whole region is 613. It is important to note here that the infant mortality in this region is quite high compared to IMR of rural Maharashtra of 1999 which is 58 as well as IMR of rural India which is 75 (see Report of National commission on Population, Government of India, 2001).

6.5. FITTING OF PROPOSED MODELS

The spacing of first child from marriage is given in Table 6.1.1, which are observed frequencies. The parameters of (6.8) are estimated which are $p = 0.322$, $\theta = 0.777$ and $c = 0.25$ and the expected frequencies are obtained using the equation (6.8) and the Chi square test is applied. The p-value is 0.06 which is more than 0.05. Therefore, the proposed model (6.7) can be recommended as a p.d.f. of length between marriage and first child.

To test the fitting of Binomial distribution for the number of children born in last 5 years, the expected frequencies (the value of $p = 0.348$) have been calculated using the model (4.1) and observed frequencies are already given in the Table 6.8.1. On the basis of these two, the X test statistic has been calculated which yields p-value equal to 0.143. This is much more than 0.05 and hence Binomial distribution fits the data. Thus, the number of children born in last 5 years follows Binomial distribution.

Similarly, the model has been fitted for the data of number of children who died during the last 5 years which is given in Table 6.8.2. As discussed earlier, the test of fitting of model (6.8) is conducted on the observed data. For this, the estimated values of the parameters are $p = 0.234$, $\varepsilon = 0.854$ and $c = 0.5$ which are obtained by using the data. The Chi square test statistic has been calculated and later p-value has been obtained which comes out to be 0.168. This value is much more than 0.05 and hence the model suggested in (6.7) is an appropriate model for the number of deaths during the last five years.

6.6. FINDINGS

The previous analysis of data yields certain conclusions which are given here. Most of the people get married at the age of 18 to 20 years and immediately after one year of marriage, they bear a child. This gives them a large span of child bearing age and high probability of producing more number of children. The distribution of space of first child from marriage follows a convex combination of Binomial and Exponential distribution. The deliveries are generally not being done in Government Hospitals or primary health centers but it takes place at home. Also, at the time of delivery, the presence of a nurse is common irrespective of the place of delivery. The people visit a hospital or primary health centre whenever they find it necessary. They have a general opinion that the facility of hospital is near to their village. In this region, most of the people have the knowledge of family planning. But, family planning methods are being used by approximately, only $1/3^{rd}$ of the married couples. Also, the knowledge of using it is lacking. It has also been seen that a large number of persons have avoided to answer the questions related to family planning *i.e.,* the people are shy about such matters.

The average number of children in a family is just above 3. Whenever, children get sick, the treatments are being

Anganwadi Centre in Melghat (*Source* – Nayak, 2012)

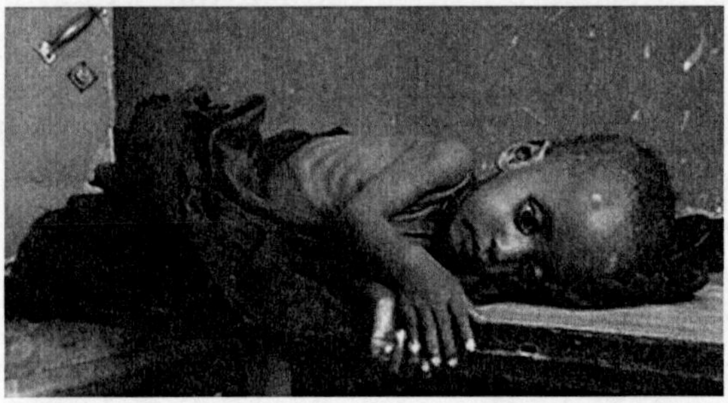

Malnourished Child in Melghat (*Source*: indianexpress.com)

taken mostly from primary health centre. They are aware about the different vaccination programs but they do not give all the necessary vaccines to their children. The vaccine of triple - polio has been promptly given by them to their children. These vaccines are being given by mostly mobile hospital, and primary health centres are also contributing significantly.

Here, the majority of the people eat mixed diet *i.e.,* vegetarian as well as non-vegetarian but they eat non-vegetarian diet very rarely. They mostly eat chickens and goats.

Mothers generally practice breast feeding to their children upto the age of at least 9 months. Also, they start giving supplementary foods after the age of 6 to 8 months. These supplementary foods are prepared commonly using jowar, rice, bajra, etc..

Here, people are aware of giving medicines to their children and moderately large population visits hospitals for the treatment of their children on their own.

In this region birth rate of children is very high as compared to other parts of the Nation which leads to a large number of live-births every year. Similarly, the deaths of children are also high in the age group of 0-5 years. That is the rate of still births, age specific deaths and infant mortality are quite high compared to the other regions of the Nation. Hence, it can be concluded that birth rate as well as death rates of children are very high in this region. The number of children born during the last five years follows a Binomial distribution and the number of deaths during the last five years has a convex combination of Binomial and Exponential distribution.

7

Conclusions and Recommendations

7.1. CONCLUSIONS

The analyses of secondary as well as primary data have been carried out in chapters 3 to 6. After completing the analysis work, certain conclusions have been drawn which are presented here in brief.

The central government as well as state government are running different welfare schemes in the Melghat region including medical aids. Still the children between the age group of 0-6 are either malnourished or dying due to Malnutrition. Also, the improvement in the status of malnourished children of different grades is not seen due to government facilities. It has also been observed that the deaths are high and numbers of cases of malnourishment in different grades are not equal.

In the Melghat region, people of different caste live but majority of them are *Korkus.* Their educational status is very low, in both males and females and generally the people are having functional knowledge to carry out their necessities. Marriages are being ceremonised at a very young age, even without completing the minimum age limit as per government rule. Their living conditions are not hygienic and their family sizes are big.

The people are economically weak. Their main occupation is farming and farm labouring which gives them little earnings. In a family, husband and wife both are working and in significant number of cases children are also earning along with their parents. Their average earning is much less. The people also rear the domestic animals to supplement their total earning. Since, their earning is less therefore they limit their expenditure too. Their main expenditure is on food only. Their living conditions are hard and considering their hard life and low earning, government is providing financial support to them.

Marriages of women are taking place at a very young age and they give birth to their first child after a very short duration. Due to the early marriages, women get large span of child bearing age which results in more number of children in a family. Generally, after one year of marriage a woman gives birth to a child. The birth of the child is taking place mostly at home in the presence of a nurse or other senior ladies of the family. Although, the hospital facility in their villages or mobile hospital facility are available to them but they visit these hospitals only when they feel necessary and frequent visits are rare. The awareness about family planning exists, but a moderate percent of people use it. The knowledge of using family planning methods is less and the people generally avoid discussing such topics. The vaccination program of children is quite popular and the people vaccinate the children for a very few diseases. The complete courses of vaccination have been given by only one family to their children but triple - polio and BCG have been given by most of the people. These vaccinations are being done either at government mobile hospitals or primary health centres.

The people in Melghat region are generally able to get two full meals in a day and majority of them are eating mixed *i.e.* vegetarian and non-vegetarian meals. Mothers have the habit of giving breast feeding for more than 6 months of the age of child and after that they start giving some supplementary foods along with breast feeding. These supplementary foods are prepared using rice, jowar, bajra, etc..

The birth rate is high in this region as well as the death rate of children and infants are also high. These high rates along with illiteracy, poverty, malnourishment, big family size, etc. cause the high mortality of children.

7.2. RECOMMENDATIONS

To solve the problem of high mortality of children in Melghat region, on the basis of our study the following strategies are recommended to be pursued:

i) Formulation of realistic, health development plans based on needs as felt by the people of this region.
ii) Need for promoting, nutritional and health education among working, lactating and pregnant women.
iii) Healthy nutrition should be encouraged through local product and local recipes.

Nutritional needs should be solved by the people themselves through a better utilization of their locally available cheap but nutritious food.

iv) Development of poultry and fisheries are to be encouraged.

v) The nutritional and health status of pregnant women need to be improved by adequate intake of nutritious diet, including iron and minerals.

vi) The program of immunization and vaccination should reach to each and everybody.

vii) The women in their advanced stage of pregnancy should be advised to take adequate rest and care, to avoid still-births.

viii) The educational facility should be provided so that they can improve their educational status. Special emphasis, in education, should be given on health, family planning, food habits, child care, etc..

ix) Better job opportunities should be generated to increase their earning and improve their living standards.

x) They should be motivated to restrict their family size and have small families.

xi) They should also be taught to maintain cleanliness and have hygienic living conditions in their houses.

xii) The delivery should be encouraged to be done in Government hospitals by doctors and trained nurses. The delivery at home, under unhygienic conditions and by untrained people should be discouraged.

xiii) There should be good hospitals in every village with all facilities so that the people can reach there within short time and avoid the adverse effects for not getting timely treatment.

xiv) By employing every possible method, the high birth and death rates should be brought down significantly.

References

Ali, A. (1987): "Food Habits. Nutrition and Health Status of Lanjia Sacra", Proceeding of the Nutritional Society of India, vol. 37.

Anderson, T.W. (1983): An Introduction to Multivariate Statistical Analysis, 2nd Edition Wiley.

Anstey, V. (1942): The Economic Development of India, Longmans, Green and Co., London.

Awlaskar, A.R. (1968): Functional Statistics in Psychology, Toronto, Mc-Graw Hill Book Company.

Bain, L.J. and Englhardt, M. (1991): Statistical Analysis of Reliability and Life Testing Models, Marcel Dekker.

Banerjee, M. (1964): Primitive Men in India, the Indian publication, Ambala Cantt., India.

Barlow, R.E. and Proschan, F. (1985): Statistical Theory of Reliability and Life Testing, Holt Rinehart and Winston.

Bartholomew, D.J. (1982): Stochastic Models for Social Processes, John Wiley,

Basu, A. (1990): "Anthropological Approach to Tribal Health", *In*: Tribal Demography and Development in North-East India. Ashish Bose, Tiplut Nagbri and Nikhlesh Kumar (*eds.*), B.R. Publishing Corporation, Delhi.

Basu, S.K. (1993, a): Study on Fertility and Mortality Trends Among the Tribal Population of India -A review, Monograph ICSSR (in press).

Basu, S.K. (1993, b): Tribal Health in India. Manak (*Ed.*), Publishers, New Delhi (in press).

Berger, J.O. (1985): Statistical Decision Theory and Bayesian Analysis, 2nd Edition, Springer.

Bern, B.J.L. (1965): A Statistical Analysis-Guisberg, Atlas of Economic Development: University of Chicago Press. Chicago, 1961, Part-VIII. Edited in World Eco-nomic Development by D.W. Prayer, Mc-Graw Hill, New York.

Blank, F.C. (1996): Hand book of Food and Nutrition, Agro Botanical Publishers, New Delhi, India.

Bocke, J.H. (1976): Economics and Economic Policy of Dual Societies, New York, 1953. *Ed.* Leading Issues in Economic Development, G.M. Meier, Oxford University Press.

Box, G.P. and Tiao, G.C. (1973): Bayesian Inference in Statistical Analysis, Addison - Wesley.

Brock, J.F. and Autret, M. (1952): "Kwashiorkar", *Bull. World Health Organization*, Geneva.

Bumpass, L. and Westoff, C.F. (1975): Demography, A Status Study on Population Research in India, (vol. ITT), Tata Mc-Graw Hill Publishing House, New Delhi.

Carlson, B.A. and Wardlaw T.M. (1991): "A Global. Regional and Count) Assessment of Child Malnutrition". l."NICEF Staff Working Paper Proceeding. *Nutrition Society of India,* 7 (37).

Chakrabarty, M.C. (1962): Mathematics of Design of Experiments, Asia Publishing House.

Chand, R. (1994): "Fertility and Infant Mortality in Developing Countries: A Study of the Relative Role of Social and Economic Dimensions of Development", Unpub-lished Ph.D. Thesis, International Institute for Population Sciences, Bombay.

Chaudhuri, A. and Vos, J.W.E. (1988): Unified Theory and Strategies of Survey Sampling, North-Holland, Amsterdam.

Chauhan, A. (1990): Tribal Women and Social Change in India, A.C. Brothers, Etawah.

Churchman, C.W., Ackoff, R.L. and Arnoff, E.X. (1957): Introduction to Operations Research, John Wiley.

Clark, C. (1951): Conditions of Economic Progress, 2nd Edition, McMillan, London.

Cochran, W.G. (1984): Sampling Techniques, Third Edition, Wiley Eastern.

Cox, D.R. and Qakes, D. (1984): Analysis of Survival Data, Chapman and Hall, New York.

Cox, P.R. (1970): Demography, Cambridge University Press.

Cox, P.R. (1976): Demography, 5th Ed. Cambridge University Press, Cambridge.

Das, M.N. and Giri, N.C. (1979): Design and Analysis of experiments, Wiley Eastern.

Dhore, M.A. and Joshi, P.A. (1988): Flora of Melghat Tiger Reserve, Directorate, Project Tiger Melghat, Paratwada, Dist. Amravati, Maharashtra.

Ferguson, T.S. (1967): Mathematical Statistics -A Decision Theoretic Approach, Academic Press.

Ferguson, T.S. (1996): A Course on Large Sample Theory, Chapman and Hall, London.

Fernandes, W. (1993): Indian Tribals and Search for an Indigenous Identity, *Social Changes*, 23: (2–3).

Gerschenkron, A. (1962): Economic Backwardness in Historical Perspective, Harvard University Press, Cambridge, Mass.

Ghosh, B.N. (1978): Population Theories and Demographic Analysis, Meenakshi Prakashan, New Delhi.

Godambe, V.P. (1976): "A Historical Perspective of the Recent Developments in the Theory of Sampling from Actual Populations", *Journ. of the Ind. Soc. of Ag. Stat.*, 28: 1.

Gopalan, T. (1987): "National Status of Some Selected Tribes of Western and Central India", Society of India, 33.

Gore, A.P. (2001): Utsav - Celebrating Statistics Education, Department of Statistics, University of Pune, Pune.

Gupta, R. (1976): Poverty and Quality of Life in Tribal Area, Planning for Tribal Development. Gupta, R. (*ed.*), Ankur Publishers, New Delhi.

Hansraj, (1996): Fundamentals of Demography, Surjeet Publication, New Delhi.

Heer, M.D. (1978): Society and Population, 2nd Edition, Prentice Hall of India, New Delhi.

Hussain, I.Z. (1972): Demographic Structure of Tribal Society, Meenakshi Prakashan, Merut.

Jain, S.P. (1975): Demography, A Status Study on Population Research in India, (V.II), Tata Mc-Graw Hill Publishing Co., New Delhi.

James, W.E. (1982): "Asian Development", Book Report-I.

Jha, S.K., Singh, S.B. and Pandey, G.D. (1988): "A Study of Economic Characteristics of Primitive Baiga Tribe of Madhya-Pradesh", XXI Annual Meeting of the NSI.

John, P.W.M. (1971): Statistical Design and Analysis of Experiments, Macmillan.

Johnson, N.O.L. and Kotz, S. (1970): Continues Univariate Distributions, Vol. 1 and 2, John Wiley & Sons. New York. U.S.A.

Johnson, N.O.L. and Kotz, S. (1970): Discrete Distributions, John Wiley & Sons, New York. U.S.A.

Johnson, R. and Wychcrn (1992): Applied Multivariate Statistical Analysis, Prentice- Hall, 3rd Edition.

Keyfitz, Y. (1977): Applied Mathematical Demography, Springer Verlag.

Krishanamachari, V.R. and Rao, N.R. (1964): "Food and Nutritional Situation in the Drought Affected Areas of Maharashtra", *The Indian J. Nutrition Diet.*

Lawless, J.F. (1982): Statistical Models and Methods of Lifetime Data, John Wiley.

Lehmann, E.L. (1986): Theory of Point Estimation, (Students edition), John Wiley.

Lehmann, E.L. (1986): Testing Statistical Hypothesis, John Wiley.

Lerner, D. (1958): The Passing of a Traditional Society, The Free Press, New York.

Madan, T.N. (1951): Education of Tribal India, *Eastern Anthropologist*, V(4).

Mandal, G.C. (1961): Studies in the Problem of Growth of Rural Economy, World Press, Kolkata.

Mathur, Y.N. (1987): Status of Tribal Health in Madhya-Pradesh, Regional Medical Research Centre for Tribals, Medical College, Jabalpur, Vol. 33 .

Mohanty, B.B. (1970): Literacy: The Input Infrastructure for the Indian Economy, Vadi Lai Dagli (*Ed.*), Bombay.

Molony, C.J. and Parmelle, A.H. (1954): Convulsions in Young Infants as a Result of Pyridoxine (Vitamin B6) Deficiency, *J. Am. Med. Assoc.*, 154.

Montgomery, D.C. (1976): Design and Analysis of Experiments, Wiley, New York.

Montgomery, D.C. (1985): Introduction to Statistical Quality Control, Wiley, New York.

Morrison, D.F. (1976): Multivariate Statistical Methods, 2nd Edition, Mc-Graw Hill.

Mukhopadhyay, P. (1999): Applied Statistics, New Central Book Agency Pvt. Ltd., Calcutta.

Mukhopadhyay, P. (1998): Theory and Method of Survey Sampling, Prentice Hall.

Murthy, M.N. (1977): Sampling Theory and Methods, Statistical Publishing Society, Calcutta.

Najtilka, S.B., Motta, T.K. and Patil, V.C. (1996): Nutritional Health Problems of Tribal Pre-school Children in Dhule District of Maharashtra.

Nayak, K.B. (2012): Melghat Syndrome, Documentary Film, U.G.C., M.R.P., Unpublished.

Ott, E.R. (1975): Process Quality Control, Mc-Graw Hill.

Pande, G.C. (1989a): Methodology of Demographic Studies, Research Methodology of Social Sciences, Anmol Publications, New Delhi.

Pande, G.C. (1989b): Strategy of Rural Development in India, Vol. I and II, Anmol Publishers, New Delhi.

Pareto, V. (1897): Coursed Economic Politique, Lausanneand Paris, Pougeand Cie.

Parsuraman, S. and Rajan, S. (1990): On the Estimation of Vital Rates Among the Scheduled Tribes in Western India, *In*: Demography of Tribal Development (*Eds.*), Bose, A., Sinha, U.P. and Tyagi, R.P.

Paul, B.A. (1952): On the Political Economy of Backwardness. Agarwal and S.P. Singh (*Eds.*),: The Economics of Underdevelopment, The Manchester School, Oxford University Press, London.

Pearce, S.C. (1984): Design of Experiments, Wiley, New York.

Pigou, A.C. (1932): The Economics of Welfare, Macmillan Company, London.

Pingle, U. (1991): Integrated Approach to Tribal Development and Health, Institute of Genetics, Hyderabad, V. 37.

Prabhu-Ajgaonkar, S.G. (1995): On J.B.S. Haldane's Conjecture about Indian Origin of Inferential Statisics, Ganita Bharati, *Bull. Ind. Hist. Math.*, 17.

Pressat, R. (1973): Demographic Analysis, Methods, Results, Application.

Ramachandran, P. (1988): Use of Socio-Economic Parameters to Assess Nutrition Status, Oxford University Press, New Delhi.

Rao, D.H. (1996): Nutrition Profile of Indian tribes, Nutrition News, National Institute of Nutrition, Hyderabad, V. 17.

Rao, K.V. and Devi, V.S. (1978): Relative Importance of Factors Affecting Body Weight in Pre-School Children as a Result of Nutritional Status, *Indian J. Med. Re.*, 68.

Rao, P.N. and Singh, D. (1963): A Study of Socio-economic Diet and Nutritional Status of Rural Community Near Hyderabad, *Jour. Trop. Geog. Med.*, 15: 3.

Ray, S.K., Yadav, R. and Mathur, Y.N. (1988): Nutritional Status of Pre-school Children of Primitive Baiga Tribe of Madhya-Pradesh, XXI Annual Meeting of the NSI.

Raza, M., Ahmad, A. and Sheel, N. (1990): Special Pattern of Tribal Literacy in India, *In*: Demography of Tribal Development, Bose, Sinha and Tyagi (*Eds.*), B.R. Publishing Corporation, Delhi.

Rostow, W.W. (1960): Stages of Economic Growth, Cambridge University Press.

Scrimshaw, N.S., Taylor, C.E. and Gordon, G.E. (1968): Interactions of Nutrition and Infections, *World Health Organization*, Geneva.

Shah, V.P. and Patel, T. (1984): Social Contexts of Tribal Education, Concept Publishing Company, Delhi.

Sharma, M. (1987): Bonded Labour in India, Biblia Impex Pvt. Ltd., New Delhi.

Simon, K. (1983): Modern Economic Growth: Findings and Reflections, Todaro, M.P. (*Ed.*), The Struggle for Economic Development, Longman, New York.

Singh, A.K. (1993): Tribes and Tribal Life Approaches to Development in Tribal Context, Sarup & Sons, New Delhi.

Singh, K.S. (1993): Status of Scheduled Tribes: Some Reflections on the Debate on the Indigenous Peoples, *Social Change*, 23 (2–3).

Sinha, U.P. (1986): Ethno Demographic Study of Tribal Population in India, International Institute for Population Studies, Bombay (Mumbai).

Sinha, I.P. (1990): Demographic Profile of Tribal Population in India, *In*: Demography of Tribal Development, Bose *et al*. (*Ed.*), B.R. Publishing Corporation, Delhi.

Spengler, J.J. and Duncan, O.D. (*Ed.*), (1963): Demographic Analysis: Selected Readings, New York, Free Press.

Spiegelman, M. (1969): Introduction to Demographic Analysis, Harvard University Press.

Srikanta, S.G. and Viswesara Rao, K. (1982): Nutrition Statistics in India, Base data on Indian Economy: *Social Statistics*, 4.

Srivastava, H.C. and Chaturvedi, M.K. (1989): Dependency and Common Property Resources of Tribals and Rural Poor, Common Wealth Publication, Delhi.

Sukhatme, B.V. (1984): Sample Survey Methods and Its Applications, Indian Society of Agricultural Statistics.

Swaminathan, M. (1985): Essentials of Food and Nutrition, The Bangalore Printing and Publishing Co. Ltd., Bangalore.

Taha, F.L.A. (1982): Operational Research: An Introduction, Macmillan.

Tekhre, Y.L. (1989): Impact of Family Welfare Program on Tribal Women, Ph.D. Thesis (Unpublished), IIPS, Mumbai.

Thakur, D. (1986): Socio-economic Development of Tribes in India, Deep and Deep Publications, New Delhi.

Thompson and Lewis (1950): Population Problems, Mc-Graw Hill, New York.

Vaidya, N. and Taneja, P.C. (1966): Nutrition Profile of Pre-school Children Belonging to Bhil Tribes of Jhabua District in Madhya-Pradesh, NIN Scientific Session, V. 31.

Vilter, R.W. (1953): The Effect of Vitamin B6 Deficiency Induced by Desoxypyridoxine in Human-Beings, *J. Lab. Clin. Med.*, 42.

W.H.O. (1963): Malnutrition and Disease - Freedom from Hunger Campaign, Basic Study 12, *World Health Organization*, Geneva.

Zacks, S. (1971): Theory of Statistical Inference, John Wiley and Sons, New York.

Appendix -A

QUESTIONNAIRE

PART- I- GENERAL PROFILE

(i) Taluka: Dharni Chikhaldara
(ii) Name of Village:

1. Name of the Head of the House

(i) Age: (ii) Sex: M/F

Respondent's Name

(i) Age- ii) Sex - M/F
(iii) Marital Status: Married/Unmarried
(iv) Age at Marriage:

2. Husband: (i) Below 12 Years

(ii) 12-15 Years (iii) 15-18 Years
(iv) 18-21 Years (v) 21-24 Years
(vi) Above 24 Years

Wife: (i) Below 12 Years

(ii) 2-15 Years (iii) 15-18 Years
(iv) 18-21 Years (v) 21-24 Years

(vi) Above 24 Years (vii) Educational Qualification:

3. Husband: (i) illiterate

(ii) Functional literate (iii) 4th Pass
(iv) 7th Pass (v) Matric fail
(vi) Matric Pass

Wife

(i) Illiterate ( ) (ii) Functional literate ( )
(iii) 4th Pass ( ) (iv) 7th Pass ( )
(v) Matric fail ( ) (vi) Matric Pass ( )

4. Religion
5. Caste
6. Language
7. Types of Houses

(i) Temporary huts made from Grass. Mud. etc. ( )
(ii) Permanent bamboo huts ( )
(iii) Parched hutment ( )
(iv) Temporary stone huts ( )
(v) Permanent dwellings made of bricks and cement ( )

8. Household information-

Sr.	Name	Relation	Age	Sex	Marital	Children	Education

Total Family Members-

PART II - DETAILS OF ECONOMIC STATUS

1. Occupation

(i)	Hunting	( )	(ii)	Dairy	( )
(iii)	Forest labour	( )	(iv)	Fishing	( )
(v)	Farming	( )	(vi)	Farm-labour	( )
(vii)	Animal Husbandry	( )			
(viii)	Collecting and selling wax and honey	( )			
(ix)	Vaidh	( )	(x)	Village Mantrik	( )
(xi)	Others	( )			

2. Yearly Income

(i)	Husband's Income	( )	(ii)	Wife's Income	( )
(iii)	Children's Income	( )	(iv)	Other Relative's Income	( )

Total Yearly Income -

3. Do you have domestic animal?

Yes ( ) No ( )

If Yes, then Which

(i)	Cows	( )	(ii)	Buffaloes	( )
(iii)	Bullock	( )	(iv)	Sheeps Goats	( )
(v)	Chickens	( )	(vi)	Pigs	( )

4. Do you earn anything from the above mentioned animals?

Yes ( ) No ( )

5. Monthly Expenditure-

Total Expenditure-

(i)	Food-	(ii)	Clothing-
(iii)	Shelter-	(iv)	Medicines
(v)	Farming-	(vi)	Animal s-
(vii)	Festivals-		

6. Is your income enough for food and clothing?

Yes ( ) No ( )

Does your income satisfy all your needs?

Yes ( ) No ( )

7. If no, then which needs?

(i) Medicines ( ) (ii) Food ( )
(iii) Clothing ( ) (iv) House repair ( )
(v) Building a house ( )

8. Do you get any type of Government aids?

Yes ( ) No ( )

9. If Yes, then for what and how much ?

Sl. no.	For	Amount

PART III -DEMOGRAPHIC FACTORS

1. Marriage age of the wife:

(i) 12 ( ) (ii) 13 ( )
(iii) 14 ( ) (iv) 15 ( )
(v) 16 ( ) (vi) 17 ( )
(vii) 18 ( ) (viii) 24 ( )

2. After how many years of marriage did you have your first child?

(i) 01 Year ( ) (ii) 02 Year ( )
(iii) 03 Years ( ) (iv) >03 Years ( )

3. Where did the child take birth ?

(i) At home ( ) (ii) Government Hospital ( )

(iii) Primary Health Centre ( )

4. Was a nurse present at the time of delivery ?

(i) Yes ( ) (ii) No ( )

5. Who did the delivery?

(i) Mother and other ladies at home ( )
(ii) Neighbouring ladies ( )
(iii) Dai ( )
(iv) Others ( )

6. Is there a Government hospital Primary health centre in near your village?

Yes ( ) No ( )

7. How many times does a government mobile hospital visit your village?

(i) Once in a week ( ) (ii) Once in a fortnight ( )
(iii) Once in a month ( ) (iv) Whenever necessary ( )

8. How many times do you visit a hospital?

(i) Once in a week ( ) (ii) Once in a fortnight ( )
(iii) Once in a month ( ) (iv) Whenever necessary ( )

9. Do you have the knowledge of family planning ?

Yes ( ) No ( )

10. From where did you get this information?

(i) Gram sevak/Sevika ( ) (ii) Grampanchayat ( )
(iii) Anganwadi ( ) (iv) Others ( )

11. Do you feel like doing family planning?

Yes ( ) No ( )

12. Do you have the knowledge of different methods of family planning ?

Yes ( ) No ( )

13. Do you practice any of the family planning methods?

Yes	( )	No	( )

If yes, then which -

(i)	Male family planning methods.	( )
(ii)	Female family planning methods	( )

14. Are the things necessary for family planning, easily available?

Yes	( )	No	( )

15. Are these things available free of cost?

Yes	( )	No	( )

16. Do you have the knowledge of using these things?

Yes	( )	No	( )

17. How many children do you have?

(i)	One	( )	(ii)	Two	( )
(iii)	Three	( )	(iv)	Four	( )
(v)	Five	( )	(vi)	More	( )

18. When sick, from whom do you take medicines?

(i)	Advice of senior people at home	( )
(ii)	Mantrik	( )
(iii)	Government mobile hospital	( )
(iv)	Primary health centre	( )
(v)	Vaidh	( )

19. Have you vaccinated your children ?

Yes	( )	No	( )

20. How many vaccines did you give to your children?

(i)	One	( )	(ii)	Two	( )
(iii)	Three	( )	(iv)	Four	( )
(v)	Five	( )	(vi)	More	( )

21. Did you vaccinate for different diseases?

(i)	BCG	( )	(ii)	Polio-Triple	( )
(iii)	Pox	( )	(iv)	Measles	( )
(v)	Meningitis	( )			

22. From where did you vaccinate your children?

(i)	Government mobile hospital	( )
(ii)	Primary health centre	( )
(iii)	Private Doctors	( )
(iv)	Social workers	( )
(v)	Others	( )

23. Are all the children in your family vaccinated?

(i) Yes ( ) (ii) No ( )

24. Do you think that after vaccination your children do not catch the different diseases?

(i) Yes ( ) (ii) No ( )

25. Do you think that without vaccination your children can die?

(i) Yes ( ) (ii) No ( )

26. What type of food do you eat ?

(i)	Vegetarian	( )	(ii)	Non - Vegetarian	( )
(iii)	Mixed	( )			

27. Do you get two full meals a day?

(i) Yes ( ) (ii) No ( )

28. How many non- vegetarian meals do you take?

(i)	Everyday	( )	(ii)	5 times a week	( )
(iii)	Whenever possible	( )			

29. What type of non-veg do you generally take?

(i)	Birds	( )	(ii)	Goats	( )
(iii)	Pigs	( )	(iv)	Chickens	( )
(v)	Fishes	( )			

30. Do you give breast feeding to your children?

    (i) Yes ( ) (ii) No ( )

31. For how many months do you give breast feeding to your children ?

    (i) 03 Months ( ) (ii) 06 Months ( )
    (iii) 09 Months ( ) (iv) 12 Months ( )
    (v) Till the birth of second child ( )

32. Do you also give supplementary food to your children?

    (i) Yes ( ) (ii) No ( )

33. From which month do you start giving supplementary food to your children'.'

    (i) 02 Months ( ) (ii) 04 Months ( )
    (iii) 06 Months ( ) (iv) 08 Months ( )

34. From which of the following food grains do you prepare this supplementary food

    (i) Rice ( ) (ii) Jowari ( )
    (iii) Bajra ( ) (iv) Dal ( )
    (v) Anganwadi food ( )

35. Do you give any precautionary medicines to your children?

    (i) Yes ( ) (ii) No ( )

36. Do you take your children to the hospital, yourself?

    (i) Yes ( ) (ii) No ( )

37. How many children took birth in your family in the last five years?

Year	No. of Children born
1997	
1998	
1999	
2000	
2001	

38. How many children died in your family in the last five years?

Year	Age	Sex	Reasons of death	Treatment given
1997				
1998				
1999				
2000				
2001				

Subject Index